SECONDA~~~~~ ̄ ̄ ̄ ̄ ̄ ̄OAN IT~~~~~TERS
AND PLENARIES
HISTORY

Other titles available in the Starters and Plenaries series:

Secondary Starters and Plenaries by Kate Brown
More Secondary Starters and Plenaries by Mike Gershon
Secondary Starters and Plenaries: English by Johnnie Young

Coming soon:
Secondary Starters and Plenaries: Geography by Brin Best and Steve Padget

Other titles available from Bloomsbury Education:

How to survive your first year in teaching by Sue Cowley
Pimp your Lesson! Prepare, Innovate, Motivate, Perfect by Isabella Wallace and Leah Kirkman
Why are you shouting at us? The dos and don'ts of behaviour management by Phil Beadle and John Murphy
The History Teacher's Handbook by Neil Smith

SECONDARY STARTERS AND PLENARIES
HISTORY

Ready-to-use activities for teaching History

By Mike Gershon

BLOOMSBURY

LONDON • NEW DELHI • NEW YORK • SYDNEY

Published 2013 by Bloomsbury Education
Bloomsbury Publishing plc
50 Bedford Square, London, WC1B 3DP

www.bloomsbury.com

9781441171931

10 9 8 7 6 5 4 3 2 1

Typeset by Fakenham Prepress Solutions, Fakenham, Norfolk NR21 8NN
Printed and bound by CPI Group (UK) Ltd, Croydon CR0 4YY

This book is produced using paper that is made from wood grown in managed, sustainable
forests. It is natural, renewable and recyclable. The logging and manufacturing processes
conform to the environmental regulations of the country of origin.

To view more of our titles visit: www.bloomsbury.com

Online resources accompany this book available at:

www.bloomsbury.com/secondary-starters-and-plenaries-history-9781441171931

**Please type the URL into your web browser and follow the instructions
to access the resources. If you experience any problems, please contact
Bloomsbury at: companionwebsite@bloomsbury.com**

Contents

Introduction

Welcome to *Secondary Starters and Plenaries: History*. This book provides you with 25 starters and 25 plenaries, all of which are specially designed for teaching secondary History. Each starter is paired with a complementary plenary. This means you can use all of the activities on their own, but can also bookend your lessons with two which are related, providing a sense of continuity if it suits your purposes.

The book has been written from the perspective of the working teacher, someone whose time, as we all know, is precious. Each activity is explained clearly and illustrated with examples of how it might be put into action. The intention has been to make it as easy as possible to use the ideas outlined in the book. They are ready-made; each one can be picked up and slotted into your lesson plans with no more than minimal adjustments being required. Of course, you may want to use the starters and plenaries described here as a jumping-off point, or to adapt them to suit your needs.

In this introduction I will look in a little detail first at starters, then at plenaries, before finally moving on to discuss the structure of the book itself.

Starters

The three-part lesson – in which one begins with a starter, moves on to one or more of the main activities and concludes with a plenary – has become the norm in the classroom in England. Ofsted expects to see such a structure when observing lessons and, because of the demands which the inspection system places on individual schools, it is highly likely that internal observations will have the same expectations.

The model has much to be said for it, although ought not to be taken as the be-all and end-all as it is sometimes presented. The logic behind the approach is roughly as follows:

- Use a starter to engage students in the lesson. This includes helping them to experience success, eliciting prior knowledge and getting them thinking in the context of the subject and topic under consideration.

- Main activities provide time in which students can engage with information and ideas in an extended form. This is where the primary learning takes place. Activities can be episodic – each of which is short and circumscribed – or sustained. Independent work ought to form a part of this section because it allows students to work actively. This has been shown to be a more effective way of learning than passive experience.

- Finish the lesson with a plenary. This provides an opportunity to revisit in some way the content that has been covered in the lesson. In so doing, the student is encouraged to reinforce what they have learnt. Returning to the material means returning to the learning which pupils have done. It is a little like standing back and analysing a picture you have just painted.

The starter then, is a student's way in to the lesson. There are many ways in which you can help them to get on board. It is a commonly held position that all starters should be quick and pacey; designed to grab student's attention and then move them seamlessly into the main activities. This need not necessarily be the case though. Sharp starters can be good, but so too can longer ones. In a 50 minute lesson, there is nothing wrong with taking 15 minutes over a starter if it is designed in such a way as to ensure students are learning throughout that time.

The point is that one should not take the structure of the three-part lesson to be rigid. It is a format in which learning can take place and it can be moulded to suit your intentions. One advantage of using starters which are more drawn out is that it encourages students to maintain attention and to think more deeply. The engagement and feeling of success which we seek can still be achieved in a starting activity that is relatively extended. Whilst it is closely linked to short, snappy starters, it is not exclusive to them.

Flexibility is important in teaching and in planning for learning; having a range of options which you can use to begin lessons is useful. The starters I have included in this book can be used as extended activities or as quick, speedy ones. At different times there will no doubt be call for using each approach.

Plenaries

Plenaries differ significantly from starters. They have a logical structure which is absent from the kind of activities we might use to begin lessons. It works as follows:

i   Things occur in the lesson.

ii The plenary comes at the end of the lesson.

iii The nature of a plenary is to add nothing new (it might facilitate something the creation or addition of something new, but this will still be based on what has gone before).

iv Therefore, the plenary must be based on what has come before in the lesson (perhaps, as well, previous lessons).

The plenary looks back and it does not need to introduce new material. Contrast this to starters. They operate at the beginning of lessons, before anything has been done. By their very nature, therefore, they will need to be based on new material (in the sense that it is new to the lesson. This is inevitable because the starter is the first thing that goes to make up the lesson).

Taking the lesson as an individual unit, it is clear that the plenary's function, operating as it does at the end, is to manipulate that which has preceded it in some way or another.

All teachers know this and are adept at realising the fact through the skilful use of various activities to conclude lessons. Nonetheless, it is worth being aware of the structure which underlies plenaries in order that we might understand them better.

The three ways that plenaries function are: revisiting; reusing; and reflecting/reviewing.

Revisiting involves students returning to that which they have learnt during the lesson. This could be done in a variety of ways, for example, by the teacher bringing up slides which have formed the basis of study or by students re-reading their own work. The intention behind such an activity is to reinforce the learning that has taken place by going over it again. Think of it as re-treading the path to ensure that it remains clear.

Reusing is a little more complex and demands more effort on behalf of students. It requires them to take what they have learnt during the lesson and put it to use. This can be in the order of application, analysis, synthesis, evaluation or some combination thereof. A plenary of this type is a more active way of reinforcing learning because it requires students to do things with their knowledge.

Reflecting/reviewing differs again. In plenaries of this type, students are being asked to take a step back and analyse the lesson in order to consider what has been done and what has been learnt. In so doing, they are engaging in meta-cognition. That is, thinking about thinking. This is helpful because it makes students active participants in their own learning and encourages self-awareness.

The plenaries in this book draw on the theory outlined above, as well as introducing some further ideas about how to structure such activities.

The structure of the book

As noted above, each starter is paired with a complementary plenary. This is not intended in any way to circumscribe your use of the activities in the book. Any of the starters or plenaries which follow can be used independently. Also, different starters and plenaries can be paired together, although this may sometimes require minor adaptations to be made. The intention has been to provide as much use as possible for you, the reader. By putting starters and plenaries together, and ensuring they fit well, the opportunity is there to take these and use them both when planning a lesson. Doing this will ensure your lesson has a strong start and a strong finish, that there is some continuity between these and, perhaps most important of all, that a great deal of time is saved in the planning process, this being increased by two aspects of the lesson being set-out, ready for use.

The activities are divided into seven sections:

1 Sources and evidence

2 Reasons and judgements

3 Interpretation

4 Drama

5 Contrast and comparison

6 Speculation, cause and consequence

7 Enquiry

Every starter and every plenary is explained and illustrated with examples taken from across the curriculum and supplemented with ways in which it might be extended and developed. The last of these is of particular use when challenging students, stretching their thinking and differentiating for pupils who are highly skilled in the subject. Another feature of this book are the Teacher's tips, in which advice is given on some of the more practical aspects of delivering certain starters and plenaries. Resources sections provide links to useful websites where further material for lessons can be obtained and Extension sections outline how to broaden the scope of the lesson.

I hope you and your students find the ideas which follow to be beneficial and that they both save you time and help your students to learn.

Mike Gershon

Publisher's acknowledgements

Thank you to Neil Smith, consulting author, for his hard work and contributions to the book.

Section 1
Sources and evidence

Starter

Who, what, when, where, why and how?

Get students thinking about the six biggest questions in history.

Topic: Personal experiences during World War One.

Materials required: A hand-out containing a source, or a series of hand-outs containing different sources.

Activity

Give students a source related to the topic. For this example, use a letter sent home by a British soldier fighting in World War One. You could present this via the whiteboard, or distribute it as a hand-out. Ask students to analyse the source in detail. Introduce them to the six big questions or, the '5 Ws and 1 H' (Who? What? When? Where? Why? How?) and ask them to use these questions to draw out information from the source. You may want to model the questions in greater detail. For example: Who is the author of the source? What is the source about? Why might the source have been created?

Teacher's tip

Any source is appropriate for this starter. Written and visual sources can easily be shown on the whiteboard or handed out as photocopies. Film sources may require repeated playing to ensure students have enough time to get all the information written down. Using objects is exciting for students, though can be time-consuming. It may be useful to provide a summary explanation or contextual information to supplement an object (otherwise, answering the questions may prove too difficult).

The activity works as an independent, paired or group task. If students are in groups, give them more than one source (or multiple copies of the same source) to ensure everyone can be involved. If different groups have different sources, you may wish to rotate the sources as groups complete their investigations.

You could also create a worksheet to help students who may struggle with the task. This should have the '5 Ws and 1 H' on it with space after each word for students to complete the question. There should be a box next to all six in which students can write their findings.

In this example, the use of a letter home from World War One will give students an immediate point of entry to the topic. Such a source is personal in nature, giving an insight to the emotions and experiences people had at the time. In addition, students have the opportunity to read into the source and make inferences, based on the prior knowledge they are likely to have about warfare in general and World War One in particular.

Here is a list of pre-prepared questions to give to the students to use for this starter:

Who, what, when, where, why and how?

- Who created the source? Who is the source about? Who is involved in the source?

- What is the source about? What might be the purpose of the source?

- Where might the source have been created? Where might the source have been used?

- When might the source have been created? When might historians have found the source? When might we be able to use the source?

- Why might the source exist? Why might the source be useful? Why might the source be biased?

- How could we analyse the source? How could we test whether the source is accurate or not?

Teacher's tips

- Think carefully about the sources you use for this activity. The best ones will be those which contain different levels of information, with each of these levels requiring a different analytical approach. This will ensure that students are able to progress conceptually as they work through the starter. An example would be a painting that contains literal representation, symbolic representation and conventions of form and genre.

- Something else that can prove useful is using the starter repeatedly with a variety of different sources. Students can collate their findings, creating a 'source-analysis book' for the topic you are studying. This will help them in the rest of the work they are asked to do.

Extensions

- Once students have completed their investigations they team up with another student, pair or group and compare their findings.

- Students use the information they elicit to create a newspaper report about the source. This has scope for persuasive and imaginative writing. It also affords you the opportunity to highlight some of the similarities between journalism and History.

- If students finish the task, ask them to work back through their answers and offer alternative interpretations where possible. They should aim to show how different explanations can be made using the same starting point.

Plenary

Who, what, when, where, why and how?

Students use the six big questions to reflect on what they have learnt.

Key question: Why did Britain go to war with Germany in 1914?

Materials required: PowerPoint or Interactive whiteboard (IWB) slide containing a range of sources connected to the lesson. As an alternative, a hand-out containing the sources.

Activities

There are a number of different ways to use the six question stems (Who? What? Where? When? Why? and How?) in a plenary:

1 Present students with a range of material which you have looked at in the lesson. This can include descriptions of and information about events as well as sources. Use the question stems to test what students have learnt. Refer to each piece of material in turn and make use of a couple of the question stems. Answers can be given individually or by pairs of students who have been given time for a short discussion.

Example

At the end of a lesson on World War Two, sources might include: a picture of a gas mask, a propaganda poster, a diary entry represented by a picture of a diary, a newspaper article represented by a picture of a newspaper and a map showing an area of battle. You might then use questions such as: What caused Britain to go to war? Who benefitted from the publication of the anti-German propaganda? Why might the author of the diary have felt it was important to record their thoughts for posterity?

---

2 Students create questions based on what they have studied using the six question stems. Following this, the teacher either asks students to share some of their questions with the whole class (who attempt to answer them) or asks them to work in pairs and test one another.

Teacher's tip

In this second option, every student in the class is engaged in the activity at the same time. This creates a noisy but focussed atmosphere in the room, with pupils working hard to try and answer the questions of their peers correctly. It also gives the teacher a chance to walk around the room and listen to different pairs in order to check pupils' learning.

3   The teacher displays a slide on the board containing five sources used during the lesson. If the sources will not scale sufficiently to fit on the slide, they can be represented by a name or a symbol. Students work in a team (either a pair or a group). They are tasked with answering the six questions about as many of the sources as possible. The first team that is ready signals to the teacher. They go through their answers while the rest of the class listens and judges whether they are right or not.

Teacher's tips

- This method is great for creating a competitive buzz at the end of a lesson; pupils are put under real pressure to apply their learning to all the different sources. In addition, the final checking procedure adds an extra layer of revision, with students carefully analysing the content of what is said in order to check whether it is right or not.

- As noted above, modelling is important in this task. Students may struggle at first to develop their own questions; modelling will give them something from which to work. An extension of this is to share good examples of questions which students themselves come up with. If you notice a particularly thoughtful question, ask the student who wrote it if you can share it with the class.

Extensions

- Challenge students to come up with questions which get progressively harder. Ask them to try and create questions which they think it would be difficult (but not impossible) for their peers to answer.

- Create a source diary for students. In this they could record the different sources they have looked at each lesson, along with answers to the six questions. This could be returned to for a series of plenaries across a unit of work.

- If students give different answers to the same question, encourage them to debate those answers until they come to some sort of agreement.

Starter

Storytime

Use the power of narrative to draw students into your lesson.

Topic: How significant were developments in warfare and technology in deciding the outcome of World War Two?

Materials required: A picture of an unusual source connected to the topic; if possible, a physical example of the source as well.

Activity

Provide students with a source. Invite them to develop a brief story which explains either an aspect of the source, or the whole thing. Encourage students to use their existing knowledge of the topic to create the story.

Explain to the students that throughout the rest of the lesson they will be testing their stories to see if they are true or not. This is similar to a scientist coming up with a hypothesis before conducting a series of experiments.

Example

The lesson will focus on looking at warfare and technology in World War Two. Students who have already been studying the topic for a few weeks are provided with a photograph of Hiroshima after the atomic bomb had been dropped on 6 August 1945, and asked to write a brief account of no more than 100 words describing the scene and how the dropping of the bomb lead to the Allied victory in World War Two.

Ask students to discuss their stories with a partner. This will help them to refine and clarify exactly what it is they are suggesting. It may also help if the listener questions the storyteller, focussing on areas which are unclear or ambiguous. Once this is done, students write their stories down. The level of detail can vary according to time constraints. It is important students do note their stories down, as they will need to refer to these during the lesson, when they will be testing their validity.

This activity also works well with students working in pairs or groups of three to come up with a story together. The key challenge here will be negotiation, as a final narrative will need to be agreed upon and written down by all.

Storytime

Provide students with the following scaffolding to help them with the task:

All stories have a beginning, a middle and an end. Use the source and your existing knowledge as the beginning. After that, think about how things might change. What might be different? What factors might influence the change. Finally, think about how everything will come to an end? What will be the final result? How will this connect to your beginning?

Teacher's tip

It is important to differentiate the storytelling you are asking students to do from that expected of them when doing creative writing in English lessons. Whilst they will call on some of the skills used in that context, they need to remember that their stories must develop from their existing knowledge and the source(s) with which they have been presented. Keeping this at the forefront of their minds will lead to narratives that are geared more toward historical interpretation than fiction writing. It is about straddling the line between using literary techniques and writing a piece of literature. The former is favourable in History, the latter is not.

Extensions

- Once students have written their stories, ask them to think about the likelihood that they will be proved true. Students should explain what criteria they have made their judgements against and why they think them to be accurate.

- Ask students to come up with a list of questions they need to answer in order to successfully assess the validity of their story.

Plenary

Storytime

Students revisit their stories and assess them in light of what they have learnt.

Topic: The Reformation

Materials required: A physical source or a picture of a source. This will be the same one that students develop stories about at the start of the lesson. The stories pupils developed as part of the starter.

Activity

Students return to the stories they wrote at the beginning of the lesson based around the source they were presented with. The teacher brings that source out again, either by displaying it on the board or by distributing hand-outs containing the source. It is expected that in the lesson students have been testing the validity of their stories in light of the new things which they have learnt during the lesson. In effect, they have been continually re-contextualising their understanding of that first source.

The plenary has two parts to it. Firstly, it requires students to explain to their partner why they wrote what they did. This encourages students to examine their own reasoning and to come to some conclusions about why they made certain judgements when others were also possible.

Secondly, they have to analyse their partner's story and explain which elements proved to be correct and which elements did not prove to be correct. This task allows each student to reflect on their own learning during the lesson and assess a different hypothesis in light of their own learning. It also provides a useful source of peer assessment.

Example

Let us exemplify this by looking at a lesson in which students have been studying the Reformation. The source that students were shown for the starter was a brief extract from Martin Luther's *Ninety-Five Theses*. If we imagine that this was a lesson near the beginning of the unit of work, then pupils may have produced stories which did not fully encapsulate the purpose of Luther's text. They may also have taken the extract as indicative of the whole, rather than an element similar and yet also different. In analysing their own work they will draw out such aspects of their thought. In rewriting their stories they will synthesise the information covered during the lesson, reinforcing their learning.

This plenary will encourage pupils to make use of everything they have learnt during the lesson for the purposes of analysis and synthesis. In the first instance they will be applying what they have learnt, in the second instance they will be using it to provide feedback to their partner.

Storytime

Students can use the following questions to analyse their first story:

- What key things happened in your story?

- What similarities and differences are there between your story and real events?

- Can you explain what lead to these similarities and differences?

- How might you develop your story differently next time?

Teacher's tip

Encourage students to think critically about their own thought processes (those which informed the construction of their first story). This is something that is difficult to do, not least because it invokes the ego (most of us find critiquing ourselves hard for this reason). The benefits are great, however. Identifying flaws in one's own reasoning, or some other such error, can quickly lead to changes for the better.

Extensions

- Challenge students to identify rules which, if followed, would make it more likely that future stories predicated on limited information are accurate.

- An interim task can be inserted whereby students make a list of the key points they feel must be covered in their rewritten story. This could be checked by a peer or the teacher before rewriting commences.

Starter

Primary and secondary sources

Students compare and contrast sources and interpretations.

Key question: What sort of king was Henry VIII?

Materials required: One example of a source and one example of an interpretation. These could be in physical form, or they could be extracts and pictures put together on a hand-out; a PowerPoint or IWB slide containing a comparison table which students can copy and complete.

Activity

Provide students with two accounts covering the same topic or event. One of these should be a source and one should be an interpretation. Ask students to think about the differences between a source and an interpretation, they should examine both accounts before making their comparison. In the comparison, students should also consider the different nature of primary and secondary sources.

Example

When studying Henry VIII, provide pupils with a portrait painted during his reign and a modern account of what the king was like in his day-to-day life. These accounts provide great scope for investigating the motives behind portraiture and the myth-making involved in kingship.

Provide students with the 'Comparison chart' on the following page to help them with the task of comparing the sources.

By filling in the information Author; Date; Audience; Purpose; Content; Language; Structure for both sources, students can create a table that will clearly show the similarities and differences between the accounts.

A second way of helping pupils complete the activity is by asking them to work in pairs; one student examines the source in detail and the other examines the interpretation in detail. They can then discuss and share their findings, together working out the similarities and differences between the accounts.

Comparison chart

	Source	Interpretation
Author		
Date		
Audience		
Purpose		
Language		
Content		
Structure		

Teacher's tip

When choosing your accounts, give some consideration to your teaching objectives; for example, you may wish to focus on the way in which different media can transmit different messages. To do this, you might deliberately pick two accounts which are dissimilar in their physical form, for example, a painting and an extract from a work written by a historian. However, thinking in this way ought not to lead you to restrict the scope of students' enquiry; they can look at the accounts in whatever way they wish and may make points and comparisons you may not have considered. Careful thought should be given to how you will explain the differences between sources and interpretations, and it might be worth asking how historians create their versions of the past. Some bright students might even be able to point out that even pieces of historical evidence could be seen as interpretations in themselves!

Extensions

- Having completed their comparison, ask students to come up with some general differences between sources and interpretations.

- Students produce two sets of questions. The first is a list of those they would seek to ask of any source they encountered. The second is a list of those they would ask of any interpretation.

- Ask students to assess how reliable they think each account is. They should support their contentions with reasons and evidence, making use of the source or interpretation itself where possible.

Plenary

Primary and secondary sources

Students reflect on the different sources they have used during the lesson.

Key question: How did Chairman Mao affect the lives of Chinese people on a day-to-day basis?

Materials required: A PowerPoint or IWB slide containing a selection of questions or categories which pupils can use to reflect on the primary and secondary sources from the lesson.

Activity

Give students a range of categories or questions to analyse the primary and secondary sources they have worked with during the lesson. There is a wide scope questions or categories you could use and it may be the case that certain lessons require ones which are quite specific.

Below are some examples of questions and categories you could use:

Questions and categories

Questions:

• Which primary source do you feel has been most useful?

• Which source do you think is the least reliable?

• Which primary and secondary sources would you advise someone to use in conjunction?

Categories:

• Best source (with reasons as to why)

• The source which revealed the most to you (and why)

• The source you do not trust (and why, including evidence if possible)

The activity can be completed individually or in pairs, with students then sharing their answers in a whole-class format or in smaller groups. You may wish to circumscribe the questions or categories somewhat in order to focus students' attention onto a smaller number of sources. It will depend on how you have structured your lesson.

Example

Students are studying the impact of Chairman Mao on day-to-day life in China. They have investigated a range of primary and secondary sources as part of the lesson. The questions chosen for the plenary are:

- Which source are you most sceptical about and why?

- Which sources might different audiences have read differently in Mao's China?

- What source would you focus on first if asked to write an essay on the impact of Chairman Mao on day-to-day life in China?

You will note that the questions connect to wider themes relevant to the study of China during the period of Mao's rule. One of the benefits of this activity is that it gives the teacher scope to focus on skills, content, or a combination of both. By tailoring the questions to suit your purposes, you can use the activity to help your students make significant progress.

Teacher's tip

The questions and categories you provide for students should reflect the relative ability of the class, as well as where they are at in relation to the subject. It is always better to start off with simple questions or categories because all of the students will be able to give these a go and you can provide more challenging ones for those who are more capable. However, if you start off with complex questions or categories then some students may disengage. It will be hard to get them back onside in the limited time you have available.

Extensions

- After students finish writing their answers, ask for volunteers whose job it will be to try and persuade the rest of the class that their answers are right.

- Challenge students to identify the criteria by which they are making their judgements. Question them as to the soundness of these criteria. Encourage students to construct arguments to defend their methods of judging.

- Create a large chart to go alongside your unit of work. Record on this chart the judgements students come to regarding the various sources you study. You might divide the chart in three and label the sections 'sources we felt were good', 'sources we were uncertain about' and 'sources we did not feel were useful'.

Starter

What's their motivation?

A great way to encourage pupils to get inside the minds of historical figures.

Key question: What contribution did Galen make to the history of medicine?

Materials required: A piece of evidence connected to a specific individual, for example, a source describing someone's actions or behaviour; a PowerPoint or IWB slide asking students to write as if they were the individual in question.

Activity

This activity focuses on human motivation. It can be approached in one of two ways: you may wish to focus on the motivations of a historical figure, or alternatively you could look at the motivations of the author of a source.

Provide students with a piece of evidence and ask them to investigate it. Once they are familiar with the material, tell them that they will be making an imaginative leap; they will be trying to get into the mind of the person the source is about or the author. Explain that by doing this they will be attempting to understand the individual's motivations.

Ask students to return to the evidence and write an explanation of the individual's actions as if they were that individual.

The explanation should cover:

• What they hoped to achieve by producing the account.

• What benefits they expected it to bring themselves or others.

• Who it may have been targeted at or produced for.

• Whether they had been influenced by any recent events or developments.

These points can be put on the board to aid students.

What's their motivation?

You could start off this activity by facilitating a discussion about what generally motivates human beings, to help students begin the task. Alternatively, a list detailing a range of motivations may work just as well:

- Who was the person and what was their position in society?

- What sort of things would they have done on a daily basis?

- What beliefs might they have had?

- What might they have been trying to achieve in their life?

- What might all of these factors have motivated them to do?

Example

Students receive a contemporary report concerning one of Galen's live animal dissections. Such a report invites many readings into the motivations of Galen and also the report's author. Students will have a lot of scope for developing their ideas and for imagining what motivations led Galen to dissect animals, and what led someone at the time to write a report on what he was doing.

As the lesson continues, pupils will come to discover that the Ancient Greeks prohibited human dissection. They will then reflect on their original explanations in light of this, rewriting them if appropriate. This could lead into a debate about the relationship between social values and individual motivation in different historical periods.

One of the great advantages of this activity is that it encourages students to think carefully about the role of imagination in the construction of history. They will get to see both its advantages and its disadvantages by using the techniques in context.

As the lesson progresses, tell students to keep returning to their explanations and re-assessing them in light of any the new information they find out in the main part of the lesson.

Teacher's tip

As shown in the example above, if you can find a source from which significant context can be revealed as the lesson progresses, there is a higher chance of initiating engaging debate. The activity asks students to reason using a combination of source-based knowledge and general knowledge concerning human motivation. Sources which might alter one's perception, as new information is brought to light, draw out some of the tensions inherent in thinking in this way; such as the relative weight given to each element, the way in which the two interweave in the argument put forward and the premises upon which the thinker's conception of each rest.

Extensions

• Ask students to pair up, and to come up with a range of explanations covering different motivations. They should then rank their explanations in order of likelihood and justify their decision.

• Ask students to consider the wider consequences of the individual's motivations. What effects might they have had in the short-term? How might they have played out in the long-term?

Plenary

What's their motivation?

Pupils use their knowledge and understanding to assess the motives of historical figures.

Key question: What was life like in post-war Britain?

Materials required: The explanations pupils wrote during the starter (detailing the motivations of a particular historical character); props which students can use as part of their drama role-plays.

Activity

Ask students to return to the explanation they wrote for the starter. They should assess this in light of what has been studied during the lesson. They should write a short summary which picks apart the explanation, identifying elements which have turned out to be true and those which have turned out to be false. They should then write a new, brief, explanation of the individual's actions, but this time as if the individual were looking back on what they had done with the same knowledge that the student has acquired during the lesson.

Example

The topic of study is post-war Britain.

For the starter, students study an extract from a speech made by a government minister. Students would review what they wrote about the speech in light of what they learnt during the lesson, reflecting on their own previous ideas and assumptions.

Teacher's tip

With all tasks requiring students to empathise with a historical character there is a risk that they will focus more on the creative aspect of the process than the historical aspect. It is very important that the teacher monitors the work of the class and emphasises the importance of including the relevant historical evidence covered in the lesson.

Extensions

- Ask students to compare the motivations of individuals in the past with the motivations of people living today. Encourage them to use the historical knowledge they have gained during the lesson in order to make this contrast.

- Students are challenged to envisage what it would have taken to alter the motivations of the individual in question. They should support their answers with reasoning, evidence and examples.

Starter

Analysing meaning

The whole class work together to turn a source inside out as a way of introducing an enquiry question.

Key question: Who was Leonardo da Vinci?

Materials required: A hand-out containing a source for every pupil; A PowerPoint or IWB slide containing the five different categories listed below (that students will use to analyse the source).

Activity

Give students a source and display the following five categories on the board:

- Reliability

- Nature

- Purpose

- Usefulness

- Limitations.

Give each student one of the five categories above. To help students, you can provide a series of sub-questions for each category, detailed below.

Analysing meaning

Reliability: Who made it? Why did they make it? Can we check it against anything else? Do we know if it is true or not?

Nature: How was the source made? What type of source is it? What does the source consist of? How is the source structured?

Purpose: What is the source for? Who would have used it? Why would they have used it? Who made it? What might their intentions have been?

Usefulness: How can we use this source? How relevant is the source to what we are studying? How might the source be able to help us? What can the source tell us?

Limitations: Why might the source not be useful to us? What problems might there be with the source? Why might the source be unreliable? What does the source not tell us?

Example

Who was Leonardo da Vinci?

Give students excerpts from Leonardo da Vinci's sketchbooks. It is likely that, across the class as a whole, a range of categories will be chosen. This will in turn produce a range of results in the class, creating a broad analysis of the documents.

When pupils have finished their analyses, invite them to find other people in the class who have opted for a different category and to share their findings with them. In addition, you might choose to lead a whole-class discussion in which findings connected to each category are relayed by different students.

Teacher's tip

You may want to use this starter to foster a collaborative work ethic amongst your students. To do this, you should divide the group up so that specific sets of students are tasked with taking on each of the five areas of analysis. Once everyone has finished, invite each set of students up to the front to report their findings and take questions. This process will create a sense of shared endeavour in which each member of the class is making a contribution and everyone is able to find out more than might be possible through working alone.

Extensions

- Having completed their analysis students are invited to choose a second category and repeat the activity. When this is complete, they can compare their results.

- Students find a partner who has analysed the source through a different category. Discussion ensues and students share their answers, adding to them if appropriate.

- Students work in a group of five. Each pupil chooses a different category. The five analyses are brought together, perhaps on a large sheet of sugar paper, and presented to another group.

Plenary

Analysing meaning

Pupils put their analytical skills to use on the sources used during the lesson.

Key question: What effect did hyperinflation have on Weimar Germany?

Materials required: A hand-out containing all the different sources used during the lesson. Alternatively, a slide showing images of the different sources to serve as a reminder to students; a series of categories or questions for pupils to use when analysing the sources.

Activity

Students are asked to review the sources they have looked at during the lesson, and to consider which one they feel is the most useful to an historian investigating the effects of hyperinflation on Weimar Germany. They do this by analysing them in accordance with some of the the categories used in the starter: reliability, nature, purpose, but with the added category of content They should weigh up the value and limitations of each source in order to reach their verdict.

To encourage student discussion, divide the class into small groups. Each group has to analyse a source which was studied during the lesson. They must analyse it through consideration of different features, as provided in the table below. Analyses are then shared through the use of envoys or whole-class feedback. Here is an example of a table you can give to students to help them in their analysis:

Source name:	Useful	Limited	Verdict /10
Content What information does the source contain OR fail to mention? How detailed is it?			

Source name:	Useful	Limited	Verdict /10
Reliability			
Is there anything significant about why the source was written?			
What might have influenced the author's viewpoint?			
Who was it written for?			
How significant is the nature of the source?			
OVERALL VERDICT			

Example

What effect did hyperinflation have on Weimar Germany?

Sources studied in the main part of the lesson can include: extracts from newspapers at the time; photographs of the vast amounts of money which were printed; diary entries or letters written at the time; cartoons parodying the situation; diplomatic cables; speeches; government minutes and so on. In each case, students critically re-engage with the content of the lesson. In so doing, they reinforce their own learning.

Teacher's tips

- Find a student who has produced a particularly deft piece of analysis and share their work with the rest of the class. When you do this, be sure to highlight the way in which they have used the categories as lenses through which to reflect on and consider the sources: this is the essence of this particular plenary.

- It is important to use this plenary only in lessons where students have interacted with a large number of sources.

Extension

- Ask students to think up alternative categories that they could use to analyse sources. Share these categories with the rest of the class and ask them to use them in the current plenary, if possible, or in a future plenary.

Section 2
Reasons and judgements

Starter

Justify X

The whole class is challenged to justify a statement put forward by the teacher.

Key question: What was life like in Ancient Rome?

Materials required: A statement about the topic which students will have to try and justify; images to remind students of the various things they have studied as part of the unit so far.

Activity

In this starter, students have to apply their reasoning skills to a conclusion which you have provided for them. As a result, it is an activity which will work best mid-way through a topic, rather than at the beginning. Students will need to have a working knowledge of the subject to which your statement refers in order to be able to justify it.

Place a statement on the board along the lines of: 'Such and such was the case'; 'The reason for such and such was X'; or 'X was caused by Y'. For example:

1   Ancient Rome was a good place to live (such and such was the case).

2   Ancient Rome prospered because of military strength (the reason for such and such was X).

3   The laws of Ancient Rome created a good government (X was caused by Y).

In this example, for each statement, students are faced with a conclusion that is being asserted. In statements 2 and 3, support for the conclusion is provided by one reason. It is up to you how complex, broad, specific or general you make your statements.

Explain to students that their task is to create a justification for the statement. They need to develop an argument, based on reasoning (but it may also call on evidence and examples), which provides support for the statement. The better the reasoning, the better support it will provide. This will, in turn, make the argument more persuasive.

This starter can be arranged with students working individually, in pairs or in small groups. If you opt for the latter, consider whether you ought to allocate group roles such as 'scribe', 'devil's advocate' and 'fact checker' to ensure everyone is fully involved.

Teacher's tip

Regardless of the specific statements used, pupils will be in a position where they have to think carefully about what they already know about the topic, as well as what they understand about constructing persuasive arguments. The benefits of this are two-fold. First, students will revisit learning from earlier in the unit, priming themselves for success in the present lesson. Second, they will practise developing their reasoning skills in a concrete context; giving added cogency and purpose to what they are doing.

Include the following information on your slide to get students started on the task:

Justify X

There are several ways to justify something, including:

- **Evidence** – such as information from the past, things which you know are facts and concepts which historians use.

- **Examples** – such as specific cases which illustrate a point, cases which show why what you are saying is true, and cases which make your arguments clear to the listener or reader.

- **Reasons** – such as reasons why the statement is true, reasons why we should believe the statement and reasons why it would be wrong not to believe the statement.

Teacher's tip

Talk to students about the nature of reasoning and what good reasoning looks like. Begin the lesson by modelling the justification of a statement, walking students through the process of constructing a sound argument. This could include examples of where an argument might go wrong, how to choose between two competing options, and when it is most appropriate to provide supporting evidence. Giving students a fresh statement on which to work immediately after will allow them to put into practice that which you demonstrated.

Extensions

- Push students' reasoning skills by giving them unusual or unlikely statements which they have to justify. For example: 'The weather was the main factor in making Ancient Rome the centre of a large empire'.

- If you opt for organising students in small groups, make the activity competitive by announcing that a debate will ensue and the winners will be the group that can make the most powerful argument.

- Provide a range of statements and leave it to students to decide which one they will attempt to justify. When they have written their piece, ask them to share it with peers who chose the same statement. Peer assessment could follow.

Plenary

Justify X

Pupils apply the knowledge and understanding they have developed during the lesson to justify an argument.

Topic: Roosevelt's New Deal in Depression-era America

Materials required: A series of statements about the lesson. These could be on a slide or they could be on a hand-out.

Activity

Present students with a series of statements about the lesson. These can be about the content which has been covered, the skills which have been used or the general experience, exemplified below.

Example

Students are at the end of a lesson on Franklin Roosevelt's New Deal. You present them with five statements for them to think about:

1   The New Deal was a political masterstroke.

2   The New Deal successfully tackled the problems created by the Great Depression.

3   It is hard for historian's to quantify the direct impact of the New Deal on the average American.

4   The USA only recovered from the Great Depression because of World War Two

5   The New Deal was made possible by splits within the Republican Party.

The students are then asked to decide which one of the following options, relating to the five statements, they agree with:

a   I only

b   I and 2 only

c   3 only

d   1,2, and 3 only

e   4 only

f   5 only

g   4 and 5 only

h   I, 2, 3, 4, and 5

Ask the students to choose one of the options and to justify their choice. This will be the essence of the task. It is possible to successfully run the plenary in a number of ways:

I   Divide students into groups. Give each group one of the options relating to the five statements. They must work together to create a powerful argument justifying the choice of option. Explain that once they have put together their argument the various groups will go up against one another in competition; the winner being that group which presents the best justification of their option.

2   Display the statements and options on the board. Ask students to work in pairs and challenge them to create a persuasive justification for each option. The first pair to come up with justifications for all of the options indicates to the teacher that they have finished. The group then reads out their arguments aloud whilst the teacher and class judge how persuasive they are.

Teacher's tip

In this plenary you will be asking students to draw together their learning from the main part of lesson as well as their wider understanding of how historians construct arguments and write to persuade. The plenary therefore sharpens students' critical faculties, helping them to marshal knowledge and understanding for the purposes of cogent argumentation.

If students struggle, provide them with the following success criteria to help them to complete the task:

A good argument

A good argument should:

• Be logical. Each part should connect to the other parts.

• Include evidence supporting the points made.

• Give examples to demonstrate what is being argued.

• Contain reasons that explain what it is you are saying.

Teacher's tip

Think carefully about the statements and options which you use. The best kinds will be those which are tailored to the specific lesson and which invite a range of possible responses. If one dominant justification sticks out, it is likely that students will settle quickly on this instead of applying themselves to the task and exploring a range of possibilities.

Extensions

• As students become familiar with the structure of the plenary, challenge them by developing more complex statements in need of justification.

• Ask students to justify the statements using a specific method, for example, three interconnected reasons, two reasons and two examples or three reasons all supported by evidence.

• Ask students to work in pairs to create three statements about the lesson. Pairs swap their statements and try to justify those that they have been given. The plenary ends by pairs getting back together and sharing their efforts.

Starter

Why might X be the case?

Pupils develop their questioning skills in order to investigate judgements about the past.

Key question: How successful was the reign of Queen Victoria?

Materials required: A statement about some part of the topic, or alternatively, a source connected to the topic; an explanation of its use or provenance should supplement this.

Activity

In this starter, students are being asked to speculate as to the reasoning behind a certain thing. It is included here rather than in the section entitled 'Speculation, Cause and Consequence' because of the primacy of reasoning in the activity. The different strands do interweave as well.

Stick A3 sheets of paper, each one featuring one of the statements below, around the classroom.

1 A statement about the past. For example: 'Merchant ships left Britain and sailed to different parts of the empire.'

2 A statement by somebody from the past. For example: 'Life on board (the ship) was tough for me.'

3 An object from the past supplemented by an explanation of its use or provenance. For example: A crate designed for carrying lemons which you explain was recovered from a wrecked battleship. (The statement inferred is: 'Battleships carried lemons').

4 An authored source such as a piece of writing or a painting. For example: A diary entry written by a ship's captain. (What is at issue here is why the source itself exists – why might it have been created?).

Allocate each statement to a small group and ask the students to think up four questions which they would need to find the answer to in order to justify each statement. This works best when individual students have to devise four questions independently, and then the whole group has to make an executive decision on the four best questions to ask about a period.

Below is an example to illustrate the activity.

Example

Students are studying the reign of Queen Victoria. Allocate one of the following statements to each group of students:

1 Queen Victoria enjoyed a peaceful reign.

2 Give an example of a foreign observer's description of Anglo-European relations.

3 Hand out a map of Cholera outbreaks in London and assert that this was made to support calls for social reform.

4 Hand out a painting of the Charge of the Light Brigade.

For each statement, students could produce a range of questions required to investigate the validity of each statement. This would involve them using their prior knowledge and analytical abilities to ask searching quesitons which are both reasonable and credible.

Teacher's tip

Stress to students that at this stage there is no right or wrong question; however, they will only be able to make an informed judgement on the issue under consideration if they ask good questions. Try to steer them away from purely factual questions and towards more open-ended questions which help them view the issue from different perspectives. Part of a historian's job is to use reasoning in order to construct a range of possible explanations. Make it clear that students are being invited to speculate, but that this speculation, whilst open, must be predicated on sound reasoning.

Extensions

- Ask students to rank their reasons from most to least likely. They should write a defence of the reason they have rated most likely and a dismissal of that which they have placed as least likely.

- Use the starter as planning for a piece of extended writing. Invite the students to research the task only from the questions they posed: this is a great way for them to review their own performance on the task. They will not be able to find much useful material if their questions were not very searching!

Plenary

Why might X be the case?

Students reflect on the lesson in order to suggest why certain things happened.

Key question: How important was the the cult of Il Duce to Mussolini's fascist state?

Materials required: A slide containing a series of statements connected to the lesson; if appropriate, the resources which students have used during the lesson (they can call on these to help develop their arguments).

Activity

Present students with a series of statements linked to the lesson. These could take one of four forms:

i   Statements made by you about the past.

ii Statements about the past made by a historian other than yourself.

iii Statements about the past made by someone who lived at that time.

iv Statements about the lesson.

Example

Students have been studying the cult of Mussolini in relation to Fascist ideology. They could be presented with statements such as the following:

- Mussolini was the first political leader to harness techniques of mass communication.

- The cult of Mussolini was a vital factor in the development of Italy's Fascist regime.

- It was difficult to counteract Mussolini's charisma.

- This lesson has seen us develop a sound understanding of the cult of Mussolini in relation to Fascist ideology.

Ask students to reason why the statements given might be the case. This encourages them to reflect on what they have studied; they will have to try and marshal the knowledge and understanding they have developed in order to complete the task.

In the process, students will be analysing, assessing and synthesising their learning. They will have to look at the structure of what they have studied and work out which parts are applicable to each of the statements. They will need to assess the elements they find in order to decide which offer the strongest support for each statement. Finally, they will need to synthesise the elements they have chosen, crafting these into a coherent argument that they can use to support the statement.

Students can work individually or in pairs. The activity can be extended by asking pupils to put forward their strongest arguments. You can then invite the class to critique and counter these while the original proposers attempt to defend them.

Present pupils with the following points so that they can test how strong their arguments are:

- Does your argument rely on any assumptions?

- Have you supported your argument with evidence, examples and reasons?

- How might someone argue against you? What would you do to show that they were wrong?

Teacher's tip

A good way to encourage engagement is by asking your students to come up with the statements for use in the plenary during the lesson. These can be vetted near the end of the main activities before being written up on the board for everyone to see.

Extensions

- Challenge students to develop a range of different arguments, all of which offer support to the same statement.

- Set the activity up as a contest in which students, groups or pairs are competing to provide the reasoned argument which demonstrates most persuasively why X might have been the case.

- Ask students to think counterfactually. Present them with statements in the way noted above. Then, challenge them to think about what needed to happen differently in order for X not to have occurred. For example, if the statement is: 'Mussolini was the first political leader to harness techniques of mass communication.' A counterfactual response might begin: 'If mass media technology had become widespread several decades earlier, Mussolini would not have been in a position to use it as he did in the 1920s and 1930s.'

Starter

Assess X

Students use their historical understanding to evaluate an explanation, interpretation or source.

Topic: The Crusades

Materials required: A source connected to the topic which focuses on a central theme you want pupils to explore; a series of questions based around the idea of assessment.

Activity

An assessment is an analysis of the strengths and weaknesses of something. As such, it is conducted in reference to a set of criteria. These criteria form the basis by which judgement is made. If it is felt that the item in question matches up to these criteria, the assessment will be favourable. If, however, it is felt that these criteria are not met, then the assessment will be to the contrary.

Explain to students that assessment is integral to the subject of History. In it, reasoning and judgement come together, forming a complimentary pairing – a unison – through which evaluation can be made. What you ask students to assess is quite up to you. It could be a source, a statement, an interpretation, a piece of work or an explanation; the range of possibilities is extensive. You could display your chosen 'X' on the board, or hand out copies of it as students enter the room. You could provide a set of questions or criteria by which the assessment can be structured, or you could leave it open for students to deal with as they wish. You may choose to circumscribe the scope of the task by inserting a word, as in: 'Assess the *validity* of X'. Alternatively, leaving it open may encourage a wider range of responses.

Example

The topic being studied is the Crusades.

Place an image of Richard I on the board and ask students to assess its usefulness as a source. Ask them to use the following questions to make their assessment:

- What might we use the source for?

- Why might we encounter problems when using it?

- Why might it be helpful to us?

- How would we know whether it was a reliable source or not?

- What would a historian want a visual source for, and does this source meet those needs?

Alternatively, give pupils a specific question which they have to answer. For example,

- 'Why might this image not be an accurate depiction of Richard?'

- 'How useful is this image for telling us what people at the time thought about Richard?'

Teacher's tip

It is important to talk to students about what assessment involves. Use the examples of peer- and self-assessment, which students will be familiar with, in order to get them thinking about the criteria they use when making judgements as they study History. It may be useful to preface the first few uses of this starter with a discussion about what criteria ought to be used to assess a certain item. The results of such a discussion could be written up on the board so that students can refer to them as they complete the activity.

Extensions

- Ask students to make their assessments from different standpoints. With the example given above, standpoints might include: a historian researching the Crusades; a historian researching visual depictions of the Crusades; a historian studying Englishness through time; a historian studying the depiction of 'the other' in British culture.

- Provide two items which students are to assess. Ask them to compare the assessments of the two items in order to judge them in relation to one another. This judgement will be in addition to those made against the external criteria.

- Ask students to advocate for their judgements. They should move around the classroom and try to persuade other students that the assessments they have made are both valuable and accurate. This could lead to a whole-class debate in which different assessments are shared and an attempt is made to decide which one is best overall.

Plenary

Assess X

Pupils put their learning into action, using it to assess a key element of the lesson.

Key question: How did the role of the media contribute to US withdrawal from Vietnam?

Materials required: A slide indicating what you want students to assess from the lesson; one piece of paper.

Activity

In the corresponding starter, students are expected to assess an item as an introduction to the lesson. Their assessment will thus rest on prior knowledge. That could be general (as in the criteria used to assess the validity of a source) or specific (as in whether Richard I really was a Lionheart). The plenary contrasts in that, whilst still relying on prior knowledge, to form their judgements the students are expected to make use of that which has been studied during the lesson. This ensures that students revisit and reuse the material that they have just finished working on.

The 'X' that you ask them to assess should therefore be clearly predicated on what you have included in your lesson. It must be clear to students that their assessments are, in essence, a set of concluding remarks about the topic, theme or area which has been under consideration. They do not need to be definitive, just conclusive within the confines of the lesson.

One strategy for assessing a key question is to get the students playing a game of 'history tennis'. In this exercise, you ask the students to get into pairs and draw a horizontal line across the piece of paper. This line represents the 'net'.

You instruct the student whose surname comes first in the alphabet (of the pair) that they will list the points arguing in support of an argument whilst their partner will list the points for the counter-argument. Each pair has to come up with six points in total, taking it in turns to write their point on their side of the 'net'.

Within these bounds it is up to you what you ask them to assess; it may even be that you wish them to assess multiple items, or to choose one item from a selection. However, a statement about the lesson content, one that asserts an interpretation, perhaps a contentious one, may prove most fruitful in eliciting good quality assessments and high engagement from students.

Example

The main part of the lesson focused on the importance of the media in influencing American public opinion about the Vietnam War. Present a statement on the board: 'The media played a decisive role in persuading US presidents to withdraw from Vietnam. Do you agree?' Arrange the class into pairs, instructing them how to play the game of 'history tennis' and applying a strict a time schedule. In order to really focus the minds of the students you should restrict the task to no more than two minutes. Use a visible timer, such as that featured on www.classtools.net to provide a visible countdown. Once the task is complete, ask the pairs to rank the arguments presented by their opponent in order of strength. Each pair should then agree an overall verdict on the role of the media in Vietnam.

Teacher's tip

The main obstacle to this task's success will be when one member of a pair (or even both) struggle to think of an argument. This issue can be resolved by introducing a competitive element to the task: perhaps asking which pair can come up with the most arguments, or allowing one member of the pair to additional points when his 'opponent' cannot come up with a point. If it is necessary for you to intervene try and avoid providing the answers, instead try and ask questions which may lead the students to think of a point themselves without relying on the teacher for the answer.

Extensions

- Provide students with categories or perspectives through which they must complete their analysis. For example: 'Assess this statement from the perspective of a feminist historian.'

- Challenge students to use thematic comparisons across time periods as part of their assessments.

Section 3

Interpretation

Starter

Images

A visually engaging activity in which pupils analyse and interpret historical images.

Topic: The British Empire

Materials required: An image connected to the topic that students have to interpret. Enlarge the image as necessary and print out on a piece of A4 paper and give each student a copy; a slide containing a question that will help students to begin their interpretations.

Activity

Present students with an image that they have to interpret. The image could be displayed on the board or printed out and distributed to the class. One image could be used, or a collection of related images. The images could be cartoons, paintings, drawings, sketches, photographs, woodcuts, tapestries, stained-glass windows, murals or fasciae (to name but a few mediums by which images are conveyed).

Below are some great websites where you can get images from:

> ## Website links
>
> - www.google.co.uk/images
>
> - www.cartoonstock.com
>
> - www.bl.uk (British Library)
>
> - www.nationalgalleryimages.co.uk
>
> - www.loc.gov/pictures (Library of Congress)

The activity can be kept short and snappy or developed into an extended interpretation. In the first case, you might give students a minute or two to look at the image(s) before taking some suggestions as to how it ought to be interpreted. This would be followed by an exploration of the image's origin or an explanation of how it connects to the topic under consideration. In the second case, ask students to work in pairs and to discuss how the image might be interpreted before settling on an agreed interpretation which they then write up. This could lead into a whole-class discussion or comparisons between different pairs of students.

You might like to leave the interpretation open by posing a question such as: 'What might this image be about?' or, 'What might this image show?' Alternatively, you may choose to focus students' interpretations on a specific aspect: 'What might the person in the image be thinking?' or, 'How might the image be said to tell a story?'

Example

The topic is the British Empire. Show an image that is an example of a British company portraying the Empire in their advertising (for example a Pears Soap advert). Display the following questions:

- How might we interpret this image?

- What might this image tell us about attitudes towards the Empire?

- How might this Empire be interpreted differently by us compared to its original audience?

Teacher's tips

- The internet is a fantastic source of historical images. To save yourself time you could download a number of these and save them onto a PowerPoint file, creating an image bank for each topic you study.

- If students struggle to interpret the images you present them with, spend some time talking them through different approaches. These could include breaking the image down, looking for themes, drawing out the narrative and making connections to existing knowledge.

Extensions

- Ask students to come up with a range of different interpretations. Explain that it is not necessarily the case that one should always settle on the first interpretation developed and that reflection can lead to different and perhaps better responses.

- Ask students to come up with a question (or series of questions) about the image that they would like answered by the end of the lesson.

- Challenge students to break down the image into separate sections (or you could break it down for them) and to interpret each part individually before using these to come to an overall interpretation.

Plenary

Images

Use arresting images to help students apply their learning from the lesson.

Topic: The Great Reform Act of 1832

Materials required: Images connected to the lesson. These will either be those you used in the starter, a new image connected to the topic, or two disparate images. It will depend on the method you choose to follow.

Activity

There are three ways in which you might use images to structure an interpretation-inspired plenary:

1 Display or hand out the images which you used for the complimentary starter activity. Ask students to think back to the interpretations they made at the beginning of the lesson. Then, ask them to re-interpret the images, drawing on what they have learnt during the lesson to do so. Explain that their interpretations should connect different parts of their learning together through the image.

2 Present students with an image that they have not seen before but which is clearly related to the topic they have been studying. Ask them to use the skills they have learnt in the lesson to interpret the image. You might need to point out that certain parts of the image are connected to certain aspects of the learning, in order to get students started.

3 Present students with two disparate images, both of which connect to what they have been learning about in the lesson. Ask them to interpret the images, paying special attention to the differences between them. Students should be encouraged to interpret why the differences exist, drawing on the knowledge and understanding they have developed in the lesson.

Example

Students have been studying the years which presaged the passing of the Great Reform Act of 1832. They are shown a satirical image from 1831 depicting the 'balance of power' in British politics, reflecting the likelihood of significant reform being enacted.

Method 1: Students interpret this in light of the detailed knowledge they have developed during the lesson.

Method 2: Students decode the image using the knowledge they have gained and then interpret it accordingly.

Method 3: The image is juxtaposed with a sedate sketch of Parliament from the same period. Interpretation would then include an explanation of why the images are different as well as the meaning they carry.

In each of the three approaches, the image is a point of reference through which students can explore and revisit the learning achieved during the lesson. It acts as a fulcrum around which their thinking can turn. This means pupils have the chance to draw all they have learnt together into a coherent whole and offer an interpretation both of the image *and* the period or event in question.

Below are five more great websites for visual sources:

Website links

- www.nationalarchives.gov.uk/imagelibrary

- www.archives.gov (American National Archives)

- www.maryevans.com

- www.nlm.nih.gov/hmd/ihm (Images from the History of Medicine)

- www.iwmcollections.org.uk (Imperial War Museum)

Teacher's tip

Choose your images carefully. Consider how amenable they are to interpretation. The best images to use will be those which connect to a number of different aspects of your area of study. Try to pick out images which are rich in detail. The more students have to go on, the more likely their interpretations will be good.

Extensions

- Ask students to identify specific categories or themes which have proved to be relevant to the area of study. Once they have done this, reveal the images and ask them to focus their interpretations on those categories and themes which they have identified.

- Challenge students to interpret what they have studied by creating an image. You may need to provide them with success criteria or an example to help structure their work.

- If you present students with a complex image containing a great deal of information, split them into groups and give each group a section of the image to interpret. These interpretations can then be brought together to form a whole.

Starter

Competing interpretations

Students compare, contrast and assess different interpretations of a particular historical period or event.

Key question: Why did football become a mass sport?

Materials required: A hand-out containing five different interpretations of the history of football; a slide containing a series of questions for students to answer about the interpretations.

Activity

Ask students to work in pairs. This starter is best used in the last lesson in the unit of work, as it relies on the students applying previously acquired knowledge. Present each pair with a hand-out containing five different interpretations of the history of football, see the example below.

Interpretations of the history of football

1 Football developed because of the industrial revolution.

2 Football was a way for bosses to keep their workers happy.

3 Public schools were the key force in making football as a popular sport.

4 Football became a popular leisure activity because it created a sense of belonging.

5 The beginning of professionalism is the single most important event in the history of football.

Give students a couple of minutes to read through these interpretations and to discuss them with their partners. When the time is up, invite three pairs to share their thoughts with the whole class.

Next, display a slide containing the following questions:

Competing interpretations

1 Which interpretation do you think is the most accurate and why?

2 Which interpretation do you think is the least accurate and why?

3 Which interpretation has the most evidence to support it?

Other examples questions that you could use

• Which interpretation is the most realistic and why?

• Which interpretation do you find hardest to accept and why?

• Which interpretation would you like to know more about and why?

• Which interpretation is the most biased and why?

• Which interpretation does not fit with the facts and why?

Ask students to work in pairs to discuss these questions. Pupils should make a note of their answers so they are ready to share their thoughts with others. Give students five minutes for this part of the activity. If any pair finishes before the time is up, ask them to note down three reasons for their answers to questions one and two.

When the time is up, divide the class into groups of six. In each group, there should be three pairs. Invite each group to discuss the various answers on which the different pairs settled. Allow five minutes. During this time, move around the room and listen in to the different discussions which are taking place. Where appropriate, ask questions and make interjections in order to move the learning on.

Conclude the activity by asking pupils to return to their original seats. Ask for a show of hands for each question, in which students indicate their personal choice. This will give you a chance to see what everyone in the class thinks. It will also give pupils an opportunity to see what their peers think.

Teacher's tips

- This activity draws together the skills of interpretation and judgement. It is best used towards the end of a unit of work, when students have covered most of the topic and so have a reasonably good understanding of the period or theme in question.

- Aim for a broad-ranging set of interpretations which give plenty of scope for defence and critique. This will make discussion and debate easier; it will lead to a stronger set of arguments being advanced by a wider selection of students.

- As students are engaged in the task encourage debate by walking round the room and advocating on behalf of interpretations which students are treating as unfavourable. This will encourage them to refine their arguments and to think about propositions which they may not have considered.

- Use the activity as a way in to an assessment lesson. Taking the above example of the history of football, the starter could be followed by a written assessment in which students put forward their own opinions about the topic, having previously studied it for a number of weeks.

Extensions

- Ask students to choose two of the interpretations and to identify the evidence that is in support of them and that evidence goes against them.

- Challenge students to come up with an interpretation of their own. Indicate that they will have to defend this and explain why it is stronger or more accurate than the five which you have put forward.

- When students have decided on the interpretation with which they most agree, ask them to create an essay plan in which they defend that interpretation.

Plenary

Competing interpretations

Students assess the relative strengths and weaknesses of two interpretations which have been studied during the course of the lesson.

Key question: What caused the English Civil War?

Materials required: Eight sheets of A3 sugar paper.

Activity

Explain to students that they will be working in groups to assess the relative strengths and weaknesses of two interpretations of the causes of something that has been studied during the course of the lesson. For a lesson based on the English Civil War, the interpretations could be:

1   The war was the result of the factions and allegiances which existed at the time.

2   The behaviour of Charles I was the root cause of the Civil War.

Divide the class into four groups and give each group two pieces of sugar paper. At the top of one of these, each group should write: 'The war was the result of the factions and allegiances which existed at the time'; and at the top of the other piece, they write: 'The behaviour of Charles I was the root cause of the Civil War.' The groups then divide each sheet of paper in half, writing 'strengths' on one half of the paper and 'weaknesses' on the other.

Tell students that they have five minutes to write as much as possible on their sheets. Tell each group to subdivide so that half the students are focussing on interpretation one and half are focussing on interpretation two.

While pupils are filling in their sheets, noting down the strengths and weaknesses of each interpretation, walk around the room, listening in to the discussions which are taking place and reading what it is that students are writing. Where appropriate, ask students questions to challenge their thinking or to help those who are stuck.

When the time is up, explain that students should display their pieces of paper on their desks. Next, invite them to stand up and walk around the room in order to read what their peers have written. Indicate that if anyone finds an argument or idea their own group did not come up with, they should go back to their original piece of paper and add it in.

When sufficient time has elapsed, pupils are asked to return to their seats. The activity concludes with students working individually to produce a written response to the following question:

'In your opinion, which interpretation gives the best explanation of the causes of the English Civil War? Use reasons, evidence and examples in your answer.'

If there is time, select three pupils to read their work out for the whole class.

Competing interpretations

Display the following hints and tips on the board to help students:

Strengths:

- What evidence supports the interpretation?

- What does the interpretation explain?

- Why might someone agree that the interpretation is true?

Weaknesses:

- What evidence goes against the interpretation?

- What does the interpretation not explain?

- Why might someone disagree with the interpretation?

These simple questions will make the assessment easier for students to perform. They scaffold the activity, making it more likely that all pupils will experience success.

Teacher's tips

- If you have enough sugar paper, use ten or twelve pieces. This will mean that you can have five or six groups. In turn, this will make it easier for you to manage the activity. Smaller groups will also result in more students having more opportunities to contribute.

- When students are walking around the room, reading the work of their peers, keep a close watch to ensure that all pupils are staying on task. This is the point in the activity when it is most likely that students will be tempted to deviate from the learning.

Extension

- Ask the groups to rate each interpretation out of ten, with ten being the most convincing and zero being completely unconvincing. The students should be encouraged to think about the criteria they would use to make their judgement.

- When pupils have finished creating their individual written response, ask them to design an essay plan to produce an extended piece of written work.

- Make the task competitive by explaining to pupils that the group who comes up with the most strengths and weaknesses for the two interpretations will be the 'winners'. Set a time-limit of five minutes and display an electronic stopwatch on the board to heighten the sense of excitement.

Starter

Categories

Introduce pupils to the idea of categories; then get them to use these as part of their analysis.

Topic: Assess the impact of the 1867 Reform Act

Materials required: A hand-out containing something that students can interpret, for example, an event, a picture or a diary entry; a slide containing a series of categories which pupils can use to structure their analysis.

Activity

Present students with something they can interpret. Examples include: an event, a proposition, a document or a picture. Alongside this, provide students with one or more categories of analysis through which you would like them to focus their interpretation. Such categories might include:

Examples of categories

- General categories: power, social relations, cause.

- Categories informed by approaches to the study of History: Marxism, postmodernism, feminism.

- Categories which are sub-divisions of historical scholarship: history of religion, economic history, cultural history.

- Categories to do with credibility: validity, reliability, purpose.

For example, when studying the 1867 Reform Act you could present students with a newspaper article from the time when the act was severely criticised and ask them to analyse the article using the categories power, social relations, class and change. Invite students to develop brief interpretations using one or more of these categories (depending, perhaps, on how quickly they are working) and then ask them to share these interpretations with their peers.

Students will need to apply their skills of interpretation through one or more of the categories. In doing this they will have to think actively about what interpretation is and what it constitutes. This is because their interpretation will not be bound up with their own opinions – it will be ordered by the categories which you have asked them to think through. Therefore, they will have to disentangle the skill of interpretation from the assertion of their own point of view. They will also have to understand the item under interpretation from at least one other perspective from their own.

One of the major benefits of this activity is that it helps pupils to think about the wider, structural forces which affected the lives of people in the past (or which historians argue affected them). It simply and effectively contextualises abstract categories by asking pupils to apply them to a specific source or event. In the example, pupils think about major categories of historical analysis through a modest and accessible newspaper article. In this way, abstract and concrete thinking is brought together.

Give students the following information to help direct their analysis:

Categories

Think about the following when doing your analysis:

- What are you looking out for given the category you are using?

- How does your category affect how you view the source?

- Why might your category cause you to see certain things, but not other things?

Teacher's tip

The categories of analysis which you base the activity on ought to be ones which students are already familiar with, otherwise the starter will be inaccessible; most likely time will be given over to explaining the different categories and, even once this has been done, students' unfamiliarity will lead to progress being slow.

Extensions

- If your topic of study requires students to be familiar with particular modes of analysis or historical perspectives, you might like to repeat the starter regularly, using those categories which students are required to master.

- Set students homework in which they have to come up with the three or four categories to be used for interpretation. At the end of the lesson in which you set the homework you might wish to reveal what it is that will require interpretation in order to make the task a little easier for them.

- Ask students to complete three or four interpretations, using different categories, and to rank these according to which they feel is most convincing. Their final decision should be supplemented by a short defence of their top choice.

Plenary

Categories

Challenge students to interpret an aspect of their learning through a range of different categories.

Key question: How far did Napoleonic rule benefit France?

Materials required: A slideshow containing a set of five different categories. These could all be on one slide, or you could place them on five individual slides, to reveal one at a time.

Activity

Ask students to work in pairs or small groups. Prepare a set of categories (five should be sufficient) that it would be useful for students to use to interpret the area of study. There are two directions in which you can go from here:

1 Display each category on the board in turn. Tell students that they must race to interpret the area of study using that category before any of the other groups and that when they have come up with an interpretation they should put up their hands. The interpretation is heard and the class must assess whether it is an accurate use of the category or not. If it is not, the next group to finish reads out their interpretation, and so on. The activity then continues, going through the remaining categories.

2 Display all five categories on the board. Ask students to produce five interpretations, one for each category, working in their pairs or groups. Explain that the interpretations must be accurate; they must explicitly interpret the material using each of the respective categories. The first group or pair to come up with five interpretations signals to the teacher, the interpretations are read out and the class assesses whether they are accurate or not. If they are not, the next group or pair read out their interpretations, and so on until the winners are found.

Example

The topic that students have been studying is Napoleonic Rule in France.

Five categories through which interpretation could be made are:

- Military history

- Social relations

- Political history

- The economy

- Personal charisma

Method 1: The categories are displayed sequentially on separate slides. Pupils race to interpret Napoleon's rule through each category. A buzz is created and the atmosphere will be mildly competitive.

Method 2: Competition is again the driving force. It is likely to be more powerful, however, as the cumulative energy which comes from working with others will push students to try and beat their peers.

Categories

Here are some criteria you can give students to help them complete the task successfully:

- Ensure you keep focussed on your category all the way through.

- Pick out different aspects from the area of study and look at these using your category.

- Connect your ideas together, showing how the category can make them interlink.

Teacher's tip

There is a strong element of competition to the activity. You must decide whether this approach will work with your class or not. It is possible to remove this element and make the task more cooperative. However, if you do decide to retain the competition, then you ought to think carefully about how to pair and group students. It will be better to have a range of abilities working together so as to diminish any risk of students becoming de-motivated (if they feel they have no chance of 'winning' the task).

Extensions

- Ask students to come up with the categories themselves. If you retain the competitive element of the plenary then this has extra 'spice'. Students may choose categories which they believe are particularly hard or difficult. This can be a good thing as it will increase the level of challenge for the whole class.

- Ensure the categories you choose gradually increase in difficulty. This will keep students engaged (because of the gradual increase) whilst also introducing a growing level of challenge.

- Divide students into groups. Choose the same number of categories as there are groups. Give each group a category and tell them to keep it secret. They should interpret the area of study through their category. Groups then take it in turns to share their interpretations. The rest of the class has to try and work out what category each group was given.

Section 4
Drama

Starter

Character role-play

Pupils take on the role of a historical character. They have to think about that person's beliefs and ideas, as well as the period in which they lived.

Key question: How far was the Great Leap Forward a success?

Materials required: A set of character cards. Each one should explain who the character is and what their general views are; a slide containing instructions for what you want pupils to do.

Activity

This starter can involve students role-playing a specific character, who would be indicative of a group in society at a certain time.

Create a series of character cards, all connected in some way to the topic being studied. In groups of no more than five, each student should be given a card telling them it represents the character they are going to role-play. Give students time to read their character cards and to practise how they might portray the role. Below is an example of the kind of information you should include on your character card.

Character Card: Poor Peasant

My name is Li Dazho and I live in a small rural settlement in northern China. I am 27 years old, and I am married with one child. My wife and I only have a small amount of land to farm on, we would like more.

I like Mao, as he seems to understand us peasants.

Once students are ready, ask them to discuss how each character feels about life prior to the main event to be studied in the lesson, which aspects of life they are happy with and which they do not like. After this initial activity, the class are in a position to study the main features and effects of the a major change to the society in which these characters exist, and can later reflect on the impact of this change on each character.

Example

Students are studying China under Mao and have studied his agrarian reforms and First Five Year Plan. Using the character cards, each group identifies the main way Mao's economic policies have impacted upon different groups in Chinese society. From this point, the students are set up to look at Mao's Great Leap Forward and have an awareness of who this measure will have the greatest impact on.

Teacher's tip

Give students time to study their character cards at the beginning, but not too much. It is best to keep the pace up and to make sure students do not spend too long dwelling on how they might go about acting in character. It is more effective for them to get into character and develop the role through 'doing it'. To take account of this fact you could give students a brief rehearsal by asking them to react to some minor event (or a series of minor events) before you introduce the main one.

Extensions

- Once the role-play is over, students are asked to note down their thoughts on the character they had to play. They should consider, in particular, the views of that character and why they might have held them.

- Identify a student for each character who is acting particularly well. When the activity is finished, invite these students to perform a model version of the interactions which might have taken place between the different characters.

Plenary

Character role-play

Pupils have the opportunity to demonstrate the progress they have made in understanding the opinions and beliefs of different historical characters.

Topic: The Repeal of the Corn Laws

Materials required: A slide containing the different characters you want students to play.

Activity

Students are asked to role-play a character they have studied during the lesson. This could be a particular person from history or a character representative of a group of people or a section of society. Here are three activities based around such role-playing:

1 Students work in pairs. The teacher chooses two characters which are to be played by each pair of students. These characters ought to have different views on or experiences of the topic studied. An item for debate is presented and students must discuss this whilst remaining in character. It is useful to give a short amount of preparation time in which students can review what they have learnt and assess how their character would most likely respond.

2 Students are given a character and asked to explain or interpret a historical event from that character's point of view. You can give the whole class the same character to play, or provide a cast of characters who are divided amongst the students.

3 Identify the character that will be role-played. Give students a little time to consider how that character would think and act. Ask for a volunteer who will role-play the character. They come to the front of the class and remain in role as the rest of the class asks them questions.

Example

The topic that the students have been studying is the Corn Laws.

Method 1: ask each pair to role-play members of the rival factions: those for the repeal of the Corn Laws and those who were against any such change.

Method 2: Ask students to interpret the repeal of the Corn Laws from the perspective of Robert Peel. A cast of characters might include other politicians, landowners, city-dwellers and agricultural labourers.

Method 3: Ask one student to role-play Robert Peel and to come to front and answer questions in character from the rest of the class connected to the repeal of the Corn Laws.

In each case, pupils will be thinking carefully about what they have learnt and how it can be conveyed through drama. They will have to synthesise the information and ideas they have studied in order to successfully role-play characters from the time. This process will reinforce their learning and provide vivid memories which will aid future recollection.

Character role play

Below are some questions which can be used to help students to get to establish the motivations of their character:

- How has your character been affected by things which have happened?

- What beliefs does your character have and have these changed over time?

- How might your character go about making decisions? What might they think about?

Teacher's tips

- Identify students who are particularly skilled in drama and ask them to model for the rest of the class.

- If some students feel uncomfortable acting out their roles, put them in a team with a more confident student. The team can work together to come up with their character's attitudes, responses and so on, with the more confident student then going on to perform these in a role-play.

Extensions

- Develop the first activity by dividing the class in half and asking students to prepare their responses together. Pairs then re-form and the debate ensues. After a couple of minutes, and at the teacher's request, one half of each pair stands up and finds a new partner. The debate is then repeated with the changed pairings.

- Extend the second activity by asking students to analyse the reasons behind their characters explanation or interpretation. Ask them to think about the motives of that character, their desires, needs, wants and intentions.

- Develop the third activity by picking a range of characters and having different students come to the front and play each one. This could be concluded by having a multiple-character debate which is sparked off by questions from the rest of the class.

Starter

Situation role-play

Pupils recreate and explore a historical event through the use of dramatic techniques and conventions.

Key question: Did everyone benefit from the Industrial Revolution?

Materials required: A hand-out containing background information on a historical event, including the characters who were involved; alternatively, a historical play script.

Activity

In the previous starter, the focus was on characters or groups in history and their reaction to events. In this starter, the characters and groups take a back seat so events themselves can be brought to the forefront of students' minds.

The activity involves students acting out or recreating an event or situation from the past. Ask students to work in groups; three or four per group is ideal, although it will also depend on what the situation is and how many actors are involved in it.

There are two different methods for running this starter:

1 Find a text in which a number of different actors feature in some kind of relationship to one another, for example, an extract from the Royal Commission into factory conditions. Give each student a copy of the text and ask them to divide the roles up in their groups and then to act out the scene.

2 Give students the background to an event, a chronology of what happened and a cast of characters. Ask them to divide up the characters and briefly consider the reaction of their character to the event in question.

Example

Method 1: Give students a transcript from the Royal Commission in which first a child and then a foreman are giving evidence. There is a judge and a barrister as well. Each member of the group takes a role and the transcript is recreated in dramatic form. Students are encouraged to maintain historical accuracy in their role-plays.

Method 2: Give students background information, a chronology and a cast of characters related to Charles Booth's investigations into poverty in Victorian London. In their groups they divide up the roles, and present their character's view on Booth's investigation and the conditions he was investigating.

In both approaches, students have the opportunity to immediately engage with complex sources. By looking at the material dramatically, pupils are invited to think differently to how they would normally. Nonetheless, they will still be analysing and evaluating the sources they receive, as well as assimilating and getting to grips with the information they contain. This will result in a great starting point from which to make progress during the course of the lesson.

Below are some great websites for getting texts to use for this activity:

Website links

- www.oldbaileyonline.org

- www.senate.gov

- www.hansard.millbanksystems.com

- www.theatrelinks.com

- www.archives.gov/judicial

Teacher's tip

Events or situations likely to work well are those which have a dramatic element to them or which include a human element with which it will be easy for students to empathise. The Royal Commission on the Factory Acts alluded to above is a good example of something which possesses both of these. The courtroom-style setting is dramatic; it is a theatrical space where power and authority are wielded. The stories of those who gave evidence can be moving and emotional.

Extension

- Students perform their role-plays to one another and peer-assessment is undertaken. Success criteria could include: historical accuracy, quality of performance and likely accuracy of the characters' interactions.

- If you have a topic in which a series of events occurred, each one affecting the next, then distribute these amongst the groups. When students are ready, ask for the role-plays to be shown in turn. This will result in your students telling the whole story to one another.

- If a group finishes their role-play and you are happy with its quality, ask them to discuss the possible interpretations a historian might give to the event in question.

Plenary

Situation role-play

Pupils apply everything they have learnt in the lesson to consider different reactions to an historical event they have been studying.

Key question: What part did the drafting of the US Constitution play in the the American Revolution?

Materials required: A hand-out containing examples of some different dramatic devices; a slide containing instructions and success criteria covering the role-play that students are to create.

Activity

This plenary ought to be used when the lesson has focussed on a particular event, ideally one in which a number of key characters were involved.

Ask students to get into groups of three or four, and allocate a character with a particular position on the Constitution to each member of the group. Tell the students that the characters all have access to a futuristic social networking platform called 'Twitter' and that they have decided to 'tweet' a comment on the proposed Constitution to their 'followers'.

Example

Students have been studying the American Revolution.

The specific event is the drafting of the US Constitution. In their groups, students recreate this, picking out the key things which took place during the creation of the charter. A number of individuals were involved, many of whom had different priorities and conflicting interests. This provides ample ammunition for students to present a particular viewpoint of the Constituion.

As groups are preparing their tweets, walk around the room and identify two or three which are particularly good. You can then invite the author of each tweet to type their message onto the interactive whiteboard for the whole class to read.

One of the great benefits of this activity is that it gives students free reign to personify key characters connected to the event they have studied. This means they are thinking carefully about what they have learnt about those characters.

Teacher's tip

You will have to provide a brief outline of what Twitter is, as some students may not be aware of what it is and how it works. Emphasise the importance of keeping their 'tweet' to 140 characters: precision, accuracy and brevity are the order of the day here! Consider the ability level of your class. If they are highly-skilled and enthusiastic, they may well be able to deal confidently with complex or drawn-out events. If not, it may be better to confine the activity to events which are small, short or self-contained.

Extension

- Ask the students to write a reply to their neighbour's tweet, directly challenging the original view of the Constitution. By applying a model similar to that of 'history tennis' (see page 42), pairs, or even small groups of students could create a 'conversation' discussing the Constitution.

Starter

Alternatives

Pupils explore the topic by thinking about different interpretations or experiences of a particular event.

Key question: What was life like in Ancient Egypt?

Materials required: Hand-outs containing information about a specific event connected to the topic you are studying. There should be enough for one between two, as students will be working in pairs.

Activity

This starter encourages students to think about an aspect of the past from a range of different points of view. In so doing, it seeks to broaden their perspective and to promote a holistic approach to historical study.

Put students in pairs. Give each pair information about an event which forms part of the topic you are studying. At this point, there are two methods you could follow:

1   Ask students to interpret the event from three or four different points of view. These could be the standpoints of historians (for example: Marxist, economic, postmodernist or feminist historians), the standpoints provided by particular categories of analysis (the social; culture; mentalities; power), or the standpoints of groups or individuals involved in or affected by the event. Students' interpretations should be presented dramatically. This could involve quick scenes enacting the different points of view, one after another, with students switching from one role-play to the next.

2   Ask students to recreate the event as it would have been seen or experienced by three or four different individuals or groups present or nearby at the time. This differs from the above suggestion because it requires students to imagine a series of immediate responses to the same event, rather than later reflections. The idea is to think about the direct impact the event would have had on those who experienced it. Again, presentation can be through a cycle of short role-plays.

Example

The topic being studied is Ancient Egypt.

Give students the construction of a pyramid as their event.

Method 1: Ask students to interpret this event from the standpoints of:

- Political analysis

- Economic analysis

- Analysis of religious beliefs

- Analysis of social relations.

Method 2: Ask students to dramatise the experience of constructing a pyramid from the standpoint of:

- The Pharaoh

- A slave-driver

- A slave

- A priest.

By working through the different points of view in turn, pupils will develop a broad understanding of the event. This will help them appreciate the nuance and subtlety which is required in high-quality historical analysis. It will become clear there is more to a single event then might first meet the eye.

It works well if you ask students to peer-asses each other's performances, using the table below.

Peer assessment table

What was good about the content?	
What was good about the performance?	
How did the performers analyse and develop the material?	
What could they improve next time?	

Teacher's tip

Encourage students to think carefully about the consequences each point of view will have for the way in which the event is interpreted. They ought to spend time analysing and discussing what constitutes each of the standpoints. Identifying the elements which make up the points of view will ensure the dramatic performances are rich in understanding and that they demonstrate how those separate parts are manifest. The contrasts between the standpoints are also likely to be clearer if such an approach is taken.

Extensions

- Ask students to suggest alternative standpoints from which the event could be interpreted. When they have come up with these they should use them to further extend their drama piece.

- As you walk around the room observing students preparing their work, ask them what they think the different standpoints reveal about the event and how a historian might combine these when writing about it.

- After the drama pieces have been shown, ask students to create a map showing the connections between the different standpoints, as well as the areas in which they differ.

Plenary

Alternatives

The whole class takes part in a radio phone-in. A historical event is discussed from a range of different viewpoints.

Key question: What was wrong with the British Empire?

Materials required: A slide containing a picture of an audience; a set of four or five standpoint cards, one for each group, containing information about a different standpoint on that which is at issue.

Activity

Divide the class into four or five groups. Explain that shortly a radio phone-in will commence. The topic of discussion is that which has been studied during the lesson. Give each group a different standpoint card representing different points of view on the issue. These could be those of historians, of categories of analysis, or of individuals or groups from the period of history which has been studied. There is an example of a standpoint card below.

Standpoint card

You are Joseph Chamberlain, Mayor of Birmingham. You believe strongly in the Empire and think that it represents the greatness of Britain and its people. You are in favour of imperial expansion and believe that patriotism is a fine emotion which people are right to display in public.

Tell each group that they must elect a person who is to speak on the phone-in. They must work together with that person to prepare a draft of what they will say, including the arguments they will put forward. The members of the group who will not be speaking on the phone-in should come up with questions to ask the various participants.

When the groups are ready, the elected representatives come to the front of the class to join the host (you!). Try and recreate the feel of a radio studio in your classroom by placing chairs around a table at the front of the class.

In the role of the host, ask participants in turn for their views on the topic. This will hopefully instigate debate. When appropriate, the host can take questions from the rest of the class (the studio audience).

Example

The topic of study is the British Empire.

Split the class into groups representing the following standpoints:

• A colonial administrator

• An imperialist politician

• A missionary

• An indentured labourer

• A protestor against colonial rule.

The radio phone-in will focus on the question: 'Is the British Empire a Good Thing?'

The ensuing discussion will help pupils to reflect on the various perspectives regarding the British Empire including, not least, the way in which it was a positive for some people and a great negative for others. As you will note from this example, the activity is best used when there are competing interpretations of a topic, or when an issue is contentious (either historically, or in the context of the time period).

Teacher's tip

This activity works well if you play up the theatrical angle. Display a slide on your board which indicates the name of the radio show (for example: The History Show) and put on an over-the-top radio voice to announce the guests. If you have the means, play a short jingle or sound-clip to herald the beginning of the show. Finally, you can print off a picture of a phone, stick it to a piece of card and pretend to be speaking into this when you get a 'call from the audience'.

Extensions

- Encourage students to ask questions of the participants that will be particularly challenging to answer. This might need to carry the caveat that they should not be impossible to answer!

- Use your role as 'the host' to interrogate the comments students make. Being in the role will allow you to press their reasoning and to exhort them to give more evidence for the things they say.

- Once you have used the activity in a couple of different lessons, invite a member of the class to be the host. They will then take over the running of the activity, making it entirely student-led.

Starter

Rule response

Pupils have to respond dramatically to rules put forward by the teacher, while all the time staying in character.

Key question: What was life like on the American Frontier?

Materials required: A set of character cards representing different people from the period in question. These should contain a picture and a brief explanation of what that person thought and believed. Use five or six people and repeat them.

Activity

Create a space large enough for all your students to move around in. This may entail moving desks and chairs to the sides of the room. As students enter, reveal to them the particular aspect of the past to be studied. Explain that they should start walking round as if they were from that period of time. It is a good idea to provide a range of possible characters or social types which they could take on – a list with basic explanations could be placed on the board.

Once the whole class is in the room and they are milling about, explain that you are going to introduce a series of rules which the class must respond to, whilst staying in character.

You can be as creative as you like. The purpose is to get students responding to ways of behaving or modes of experience which would have been the case during the period being studied.

Example

The topic is the American Frontier during the mid-nineteenth century.

Character list: Sheriff; Cowboy; Gold Prospector; Child; Native American.

Assign each student a character.

As the pupils move round the room call out the following rules:

- It is a norm to see the frontier as a place of individualism.

- Only a small percentage of gold prospectors actually found any gold.

- It would have been unlikely for Native Americans to live in towns founded by settlers.

In this activity, there is great scope for introducing students to different elements of the past in a way which is fun and immediately engaging. It is a good idea to develop a collection of rules in advance (between five and seven is usually enough) to pick out key features with which you want pupils to be familiar.

Base your rules on anything that is indicative of the period you are studying, exemplified below.

Rules

- A rule based on the way in which different social groups would have interacted with one another.

- A rule based on norms.

- A rule based on expectations of gender or age relations.

- A rule based on a statistical fact.

- A rule based on changes in technology.

- A rule based on people's changing beliefs at the time.

- A rule based on power relations in society at the time.

Teacher's tip

By planning the rules carefully you can create a fairly realistic experience. Consider carefully which characters to give to students to help them really imagine how different life at the time was compared to today. Spend a bit of time trialling different combinations of rules and characters until you feel confident that the teaching points you wish to make will be accessible. If you feel some students might struggle with the complexity of the task, introduce it by focussing on areas that they have already studied in depth. This could be as a starter for a revision lesson or an end-of-unit assessment lesson.

Extensions

- If you base the starter on a period that students are already familiar with, then you can choose some pupils to take on your role and call out the rules. You might even set as homework the task of coming up with a list of possible rules to which the rest of the class would have to respond.

- Give specific roles to students as they enter the room, rather than letting them choose. This will allow you to set up situations in which students experience aspects of the past which they might otherwise have not been able to access (such as the experience of a group whose behaviour was heavily circumscribed by those people in society who were more powerful than them).

- Connect together a series of rules. For example: 'People explained natural disasters through reference to God rather than to science' could be followed by 'There was a major natural disaster during the period which people talked about at length.'

Plenary

Rule response

Students take it in turns to set rules which the class must respond to while remaining in character.

Key question: How far did the Black Death affect life in England?

Materials required: Blank pieces of paper. There should be enough so that each pair can have one.

Activity

This plenary is similar to the previous starter except the important difference that it is the students who come up with the rules to which a response must be made, not you. As in the starter, you will need to clear a space large enough to accommodate all students; one that allows them sufficient room to move around the room.

Put students in pairs and give each pair a piece of paper. Explain to the class that they will shortly be walking around the room whilst you call out rules to which they must respond. These rules will be indicative of the topic which you have been studying during the lesson. They can be norms, laws, conventions of class, gender or age, commonplace ways of behaving, based on statistical facts and so on. Tell each pair they must write their own rule, being sure to keep it secret. Once they have done this they should indicate to the teacher, who will collect in the rules.

Students then begin to walk around the room. Shuffle the rules, pick one out at random and read it out. Read through the rule in your head before reading it aloud to make sure it is apt and makes sense. Students have to respond to the rule. This is repeated for as long as is practicable. Finally, it may prove fruitful to revisit some of the rules which were read out and ask the authors to explain the reasoning behind their rule.

Example

The topic is the Black Death. Pupils get into pairs and each pair receives a slip of paper on which they write a rule which connects to the topic. They could come up with rules such as:

- A rule indicating what percentage of the population died during the Black Death.

- A rule about the social relations between rich and poor.

- A rule concerning the attire and behaviour of doctors.

- A rule stating a religious norm of the period.

- A rule stating a law of the period.

Use the following pointers to help students come up with really good rules:

Making the rules

- Think about what was special about the period.

- Consider how people lived at the time and how their lives differed.

- Think about what controls there were on people's behaviour at the time.

Teacher's tip

If you read out a rule and students appear somewhat bewildered as to how to respond there are two solutions available. First, if there is a student who has responded accurately, draw attention to them and encourage others to copy. Second, give a brief demonstration yourself of how to act out a response to the rule.

Extensions

- You may want to divide the class up so as to ensure a range of different rules. This could entail putting students in pairs but splitting the pairs into three sets. Set one would write rules based on norms; set two would write rules based on laws; set three would write rules based on social relations. This is indicative and you would have to decide the categories and the number of sets.

- Change the pace at which you read the rules out. Vary it from fast to slow and back again. This will cause students to pay close attention to the content of the rules.

- Insert some rules which are not indicative of the topic. Explain to students that these will be intermingled with the correct rules and that they must spot the fallacies and indicate when they arise.

Section 5
Contrast and comparison

Starter

Contrasting perspectives

Students compare and contrast different perspectives on the same topic, helping them to develop a broad understanding of the matter in question.

Key question: How far did the lives of Native Americans change during the eighteenth and nineteenth centuries?

Materials required: A hand-out containing two contrasting perspectives on the topic in question; enough for each student to have one; alternatively, two hand-outs, with one perspective on each. Pairs receive both of these.

Activity

Present students with two contrasting perspectives on the same topic. These can be the perspectives of individuals from the past, or of historians interpreting the past. For example, if the topic of the lesson was the lives of Native Americans during the eighteenth and nineteenth centuries, you could present students one source that records the thoughts of a settler and one that records the thoughts of a Native American. Ideally, these sources will refer to the same event, experience or theme.

Ask pupils to analyse these perspectives and to identify the similarities and differences between them. Once they have done this, ask them to summarise their findings and to offer some sort of explanation for what they have found.

Another way to run this activity is to start by putting students in pairs and then, give each member of the pair one of the two contrasting perspectives, telling them not to show their partner their assigned perspective. Then ask the students to analyse the perspective they have been given separately, creating a summary of their findings and an explanation as to why these might be the case. Once they have done this, tell the students to take it in turns in their pairs to outline their results to one another. A discussion ensues in which the perspectives are contrasted and pupils attempt to draw out the similarities and differences, as well as why these might happen to be the case.

The student's feedback could then inform a whole-class debate, or they could be tested by students in the main body of the lesson. If used in the latter sense, they ought to form the basis of an investigation. This could be student-led or directed by the teacher depending on the class in question.

Below are some questions to help students analyse the sources:

Contrasting perspectives

- What similarities can you identify?

- What differences can you find?

- Why might similarities or differences exist in the first place?

- How might different experiences have led to different perspectives?

- Is there any way of judging which perspective is most accurate or reliable?

Teacher's tip

This activity can be useful for revealing power relations both in the past and in the writing of history. For example, a comparison of the perspectives provided by a British colonial administrator and a citizen of the country which was under British rule would go some way to showing how power operated in that specific time and space. It might also allude to the influence such groups of people would have had in any subsequent histories which might have been written about the period.

Extensions

- Provide students with three or four perspectives and ask them to contrast these. This will make the task more challenging. It may also lead to students viewing the thing which the perspectives are about more critically. This is because they will be thinking through a wider range of standpoints, all of which may have some truth in them.

- Present the perspectives of two historians whose work is separated by a long period of time. This will get students to reflect on issues of historiography. They will be required to analyse the way in which explanations of historical events can change through different ages.

- Students who show good ability may be able to contrast a collection of primary and secondary perspectives. The difficulty in such a task comes from the different levels at which analysis must operate and from the lack of direct comparison between some of the items. Nonetheless, the results can be well worth the effort needed to obtain them.

Plenary

Contrasting perspectives

Pupils use their learning to create a range of different perspectives dealing with the topic of study.

Key question: Did everyone benefit from the boom in 1920s America?

Materials required: Eight sheets of A3 or sugar paper (enough for one per group); a slide containing instructions about what you want students to do.

Activity

Put students in groups of three or four. For this activity, groups recall or create two or three different perspectives on the current topic; in the case of recollection, it may be that you have studied different viewpoints or interpretations during the lesson and you want students to think about them; in the case of creation, it may be that you are asking students to develop their ideas out of what they have learnt.

For example, in a lesson studying the different experiences people had during the 'Roaring 20s' in the USA, ask students to contrast the perspectives of a rich businessman, a middle-class city dweller, a farm owner, a farm labourer and an immigrant who has recently moved to the countryside, asking them to either recall the viewpoints from when they explicitly learnt them, or asking them to develop what they might think the different viewpoints would be.

In their groups, ask students to contrast the viewpoints and to draw out any similarities and differences between them. Groups should seek to explain the similarities and differences they find, drawing on whatever knowledge they deem appropriate.

Such an activity encourages students to reflect on and revisit all they have studied during the lesson (and beyond). The contrasts they draw help to develop their understanding of the content. The explanations they give aid the development of their reasoning and cause them to empathise with those who lived through the period.

Provide students with the following success criteria to ensure they do well on the task:

Contrasting perspectives

- Highlight the similarities and differences between the perspectives.

- Identify any patterns or trends running through the perspectives.

- Provide a summary in which you say which perspective you believe to be the most reasonable.

Teacher's tip

The activity is best suited to topics in which there are a range of perspectives, some of which clearly differ. Using the plenary with topics which have a limited number of perspectives, or around which there is widespread consensus, will result in students not being sufficiently challenged. There will not be enough analysis for them to do. This will lead to disengagement and a lack of quality work being produced.

Extensions

- Make the activity dramatic by asking for a group of students to role-play the different perspectives in front of the class. Each time a new perspective is role-played, ask the remaining students to contrast it to the previous one and to explain why the similarities and differences happen to be as they are.

- An alternative approach is to get students to draw grids or tables in which they can insert the perspectives along with the similarities and differences they exhibit. This offers a different way of going about the analysis and presenting the findings.

- Ask students to evaluate which is of greater significance – the similarities or the differences between the perspectives.

Starter

Compare your findings

Pupils use collaborative questioning to introduce a topic and develop source skills.

Key question: What was distinctive about the Renaissance?

Materials required: Five different sources. Each one should be on a separate hand-out. There should be enough sources so that each group can receive two of the five.

Activity

This activity promotes cooperation as it requires students to work together in order to advance their own understanding of a topic. The comparisons which take place are between students' answers, rather than different aspects or interpretations of the past.

Before the lesson prepare five sources that are all about the same topic. Give each student a different source and ask them to read it carefully. They then have to think of questions about the source which they would like another student to answer. These questions could relate to the meaning of particular phrases or words in the text, information about an event, person or place referred to, or more generally about the usefulness and reliability of the source.

After writing the questions on the source, they swap their source with a neighbour's and answer as many of the questions they are able to. For questions requiring additional research, the teacher may want to allow the students access to background materials or explain that an opportunity to research the answers will be provided through the work to be done in the lesson.

It is advisable to model the type of questions which they are to ask. Once the students have started to answer the questions pay attention to those who may be spending too long trying to find answers to factual questions: the main focus of the task is to develop skills in source analysis.

Extensions

- Ask students to identify one person they interacted with who they think posed particularly good questions, which helped them gain a more secure understanding of the source. Students then explain the reasons for their choice and how their own work compared to the work of the other pupil.

- Encourage students to extend and edit their own questions as a result of the other work they come into contact with.

Plenary

Compare your findings

Students summarise their learning, discuss this with their peers, and then further refine their work.

Key question: What were the main effects of the Suez Crisis?

Materials required: Table in which to write conclusions; a slide containing instructions and success criteria.

Activity

This activity is sub-titled *Show me yours and I'll show you mine*. Ask the students to write three main effects of the event studied during the lesson. They are then told that to gain a full picture of the event's effects they have to collaborate with their classmates. This will involve them approaching one person at a time and offering them one of their effects, which they have written on their table already, getting one back from the person they have approached. Their task is to obtain at least three other effects through this method. Below is an example table.

Example

My ideas	Presents

In the lesson covering the 1956 Suez Crisis, you could ask the students to come up with the results for one particular country, such as Great Britain and ask them to seek out another 'country' in order to gain a wider sense of the ways in which some countries were winners or losers from the crisis. Give the students a clearly defined period of time, no more than five minutes, to track down three other reasons.

Once the time is up, the students can reflect on what the biggest effects of the crisis were, and who gained/suffered the most.

Teacher's tip

There are two main problems which you will need to be aware of when doing this activity. Firstly, some students will struggle to come up with many points of their own. To pre-empt this, you could put some questions on the board as a prompt, or get them to work with another student. The second problem relates to classroom management. Giving the students an opportunity to wander round the classroom looking for different people to work with can lead to a large amount of possibly off-topic chatter, and can lead to issues of large numbers of students gathering in quite cramped spaces. Again, it is critical that you pre-empt these potential issues by establishing your criteria for success right at the start and establishing your ground rules for how everyone is to conduct themselves. Once the activity is underway, you will probably have to discreetly move people around so they see sufficient pupils to complete the task.

Extension

• Ask the students to categorise the main effects: military; territory; political; economic.

Starter

Comparisons across time

Students use their existing historical knowledge to help analyse a new topic.

Key question: How did mass communication develop in the nineteenth and twentieth centuries?

Materials required: A hand-out containing a source or description connected to the topic of study; a slide containing a table headed 'similarities' and 'differences'. This could contain one entry for each column to help pupils get started.

Activity

Present students with a source, a historical event, or a description of something from the period you are studying. Alternatively, you could present them with a video clip; this is a good way to start the lesson and really engages students. Ask them to compare whatever you have indicated with something from another historical period. They should choose a period about which they have some knowledge and understanding.

Tell students to divide their analysis into similarities and differences. Another option is for students to use a series of questions to analyse the two items. Questions might include:

• Who was involved?

• How did the item affect people?

• Why is it worthy of study?

The results of the student's analysis should be written up in a table, with a row for each category and a column for each of the things being compared.

Finally, you may provide students with some themes on which you would like them to focus in their comparison. For example: attitudes, causes or constituents. Making thematic comparisons across time can be particularly good for helping students to think about continuity and change.

Below is a worked example, showcasing the first method:

Example

The unit of work is concerned with the development of mass communication in the nineteenth and twentieth centuries. Students are shown a video of one of the first television broadcasts ever made. They are asked to compare this to their knowledge of how religious imagery was used before the Reformation. They may produce something such as the following:

Similarities	Differences
Use of colour and design to engage the audience.	Moving images in television but still images in religious imagery.
The creator of the media is trying to communicate to the audience.	The content of television is broad; the content of religious imagery is narrow.
Symbolic meaning. Certain symbols are used to indicate specific things; many of which are difficult to show any other way.	Television is usually watched at home in small groups. Religious imagery would usually be seen in church by a lot of people together.

Below are five great websites you can use to access video sources; they work really well with this activity:

Website links

- www.youtube.com

- www.archive.org

- www.bbcmotiongallery.com

- www.gettyimages.co.uk

- www.britishpathe.com

Teacher's tip

If you are concerned students might struggle to make their own comparisons, provide examples for them. They are then left to focus on the analysis, and do not have to spend time identifying appropriate material with which to make their comparisons. In providing the comparisons yourself you can also select ones where the analysis is likely to prove fruitful.

Extensions

- Ask students to make a series of comparisons which draw out change or continuity over time in relation to the particular thing you first introduced.

- Ask students to make two comparisons, one of which shows major differences and one of which shows major similarities. Encourage them to use their findings in order to give a nuanced explanation of the nature of the particular thing you first introduced.

- Ask students to pick out a specific element of the thing which you have introduced (using our example above, we could pull out the development of new technologies as a specific element) and then to compare the influences on this (or leading to this) with the influences on similar elements of other events in the past (for example, compare the influences which lead to new media technology in the 1900s with the influences which led to new technologies in the 1800s).

Plenary

Comparisons across time

Encourage pupils to think holistically by asking them to compare their learning with what they know about a different period of history.

Key question: How far was collectivisation in the USSR a success?

Materials required: A slide containing instructions about what the teacher wants students to do; if appropriate, information which has been used through the course of the lesson. Students can use this to help them with their comparisons, rather than just relying on their memory.

Activity

This activity involves you identifying a period or event in history that you know the class has already studied and then asking them to compare it with the topic being studied in the present lesson. This is a good activity if you want student to identify certain similarities and differences which you feel it is important to be aware; it could be that a thematic approach is being taken and the you want students to think through a particular category; or, it could be that you have in mind a specific learning point which they feel the comparison will illustrate.

Below are some examples of how you might run the activities if the lesson was based on Stalinist Russia:

Example

You might want students to compare Stalin's collectivisation with Tsarist agricultural reforms. This would help students to think thematically about the relationship between rulers and the ruled, as well as to give consideration to the particular issues surrounding agriculture in a country such as Russia. Coming at the end of a lesson, it would also give pupils the opportunity to recontextualise their learning in relation to that which they already know about.

Below are a set of questions to help structure students' analysis:

- What key points can you identify from the period of study?

- How do these compare with what you know about another period of history?

- What similarities and differences are there between the two periods?

- What are the causes of these similarities?

- What might be the consequences of these differences for the people involved?

Teacher's tip

Ensure you have a sound understanding of your students' historical knowledge. If you ask for a certain comparison to be made and then find that students do not know about the period or event you ask them to consider, then the activity will quickly fall flat (and be difficult to recover).

Extensions

- Ask students to review what they have learnt in the lesson and to pick out a relevant theme which they might use to make a comparison across time. Once you have checked the theme is apt, ask them to go on and make the analysis.

- Challenge students to identify a historical example which accords closely to that which has been studied during the lesson.

- Give students a historical period or event which, at first glance, appears to bear little relation to that which has been studied in the lesson. Challenge pupils to compare the two items and to find similarities between them.

Section 6

Speculation, cause and consequence

Starter

Defend your consequence

Pupils are challenged to defend a consequence; they must call on all their historical skills in order to do so.

Key question: What were the main effects of the French Revolution?

Materials required: A series of consequences written out on slips of paper; a slide explaining to students that they will have to defend their consequences. You could also include a bullet point list of tips to help pupils.

Activity

As students enter the room, give them a consequence on a piece of paper; the consequence should be something which it is claimed was caused by an event which you have studied in the previous lesson. Give students a short period of time in which to construct a defence for the suggestion that their consequence is the single most important consequence of the event.

Initially, each student works in a pair, but in the second part of the activity, two pairs are merged. It should runs as follows:

- Student A has thirty seconds to tell student B why their consequence was the most significant.

- Student B then tells student A why their consequence was the most significant.

- At this point, two pairs are merged.

- Student A explains to students C and D why student B thought their consequence was the most significant.

- This exercise continues in this manner, with each student presenting the case which they listened to in their pairs, NOT the one they first articulated in their pair.

As well as forcing students to argue a case, this activity develops the listening skills of students and provides a good opportunity for peer assessment. If student A fails to present B's case correctly, then B can intervene and provide feedback.

Here is an example set of consequences based on the French Revolution:

- The founding of the French Republic.

- The murder of many French people.

- The assertion of the primacy of individual rights.

- A number of European wars started soon after involving the French.

- The eventual emergence of Napoleon.

- The revolution provided inspiration for subsequent revolutionaries over the next two hundred years.

- The first political articulation of conservatism in Britain (by Burke).

Each of these are printed on a separate slip of paper. Students are given one as they enter the room. They then take it in turns to defend their consequence, attempting to persuade their peers that it should be seen as most important.

Resources

Here are a set of questions to display while students are developing their defences:

- Why is your consequence important?

- What are the short-term and long-term effects of your consequence?

- Who would your consequence have affected?

- How would the world have been different if your consequence had not happened?

- Why is your consequence more important than other consequences?

Teacher's tip

As noted, try to provide a range of consequences. This will make it easier to create an adversarial debate. Also, it will encourage the class as a whole to look at all the aspects of the event which you have been studying. These will then be brought out in the mini-pleanary at the end of the starter activity, regardless of what their particular consequence was.

Extensions

- Ask students to create a list of the evidence which they feel supports their consequence. This could be presented in conjunction with the arguments they construct.

- When the students are working in pairs or in their merged groups, they can be given an opportunity to ask questions of each other after listening to each case.

Plenary

Defend your consequence

Pupils use their learning to develop and defend a range of possible consequences connected to the topic of study.

Key question: What were the main effects of the creation of the welfare state in Great Britain?

Materials required: A slide containing a range of possible consequences connected to the topic of study. Alternatively, a set of slips of paper containing different consequences. These will be given to different groups.

Activity

This plenary encourages students to speculate about the consequences of that which they have studied (or an aspect of it). There are two ways in which it can be conducted:

1 Provide students with a range of possible consequences which might have come about as a result of the topic you have studied during the lesson. The consequences could be distributed throughout the whole class (and therefore will include duplicates), given to groups (each group being given a single consequence) or given out in groups (each group receives one copy of each of the consequences). Students either defend their consequences individually (as in the first and third cases) or as a group (as in the second case). Consequences do not need to be historically accurate (though do flag this up to students) as the activity can be focussed purely on reasoning. However, if you do opt for accurate consequences then you should ask students to defend their consequence as being the one which should be seen as of greatest importance.

2 Ask students to invent and defend possible consequences of that which they have studied. These could be compared to historical fact in the next lesson. Students should be placed in groups once they have written their defences. They will then take it in turns to try and persuade their peers of the likelihood of their consequence.

Here is an example to illustrate the activity:

Example

In the lesson students have been studying the creation of the British Welfare State.

Such a topic has great scope for the imagining of possible consequences. To exemplify the first case outlined on the previous page, you might provide students with the following (real) consequences: there was a significant rise in living standards; healthcare came to be seen as a right; Britain's workforce became better educated; society became more equal; the role of government greatly increased after the war. These are distributed to groups, individuals or within groups and students write defences of them, calling on what they have learnt during the lesson. The task involves pupils consolidating their existing knowledge and understanding as well as developing more nuanced reasoning.

To exemplify the second case outlined, we can imagine that pupils would come up with their own selection of consequences – some the same as those above, some different. The teacher would then divide the class into groups of four or five and give each students one minute in which to defend their consequence to their peers. Each group would then vote on who they thought was most persuasive and why.

Resources

Here are some tips you can provide to pupils to help them write their defences:

- A good defence rests on evidence, examples and reasons.

- If you wish, you can attack other consequences in your defence.

- Try to anticipate criticisms which other people might make of your consequence.

Teacher's tip

Stress to students the importance of using what they have learnt in the lesson in the construction of their defences. It is this revisiting and reconstituting of the lesson content which sets this activity apart from its complementary starter, making it stand out as a plenary in its own right.

Extensions

- Challenge students to write out a complete chain of reasoning which connects their consequence with the thing which has been said to cause it. Ask them to make each step as small as possible (this increases the difficulty).

- Encourage students to include as much as possible from the lesson in their defences. This will entail pupils analysing what they have learnt so as to work out how to subjugate it to the demands of their argument.

- Once students have defended their consequences, ask them to swap over and try defending a different one. The sudden change of perspective can be quite challenging.

Starter

Sell your cause

Students work in groups to create a sales pitch explaining why a particular cause is the best explanation of a historical event.

Key question: Why did the the War of the Roses start?

Materials required: A hand-out containing an event and a series of causes which contributed to that event; a slide containing instructions and success criteria about how groups are to 'sell' their cause.

Activity

This starter is best used when students already have knowledge of some particular event. It works well as a refresher, getting students to think carefully about some part of the past which you might have covered with them in their previous lesson.

1 Place an event on the board along with a series of causes which it has been said contributed to that event occurring. Put students in pairs or threes and assign one of the causes to each group. Explain that the task is to 'sell' the cause assigned through a short speech, television advertisement or sales pitch.

2 Students work in their groups to create one of the options previously noted. Once the time is up, groups either sell to one another or to the whole class. In the first case, groups could pair up and take it in turns to make their speech, advert or sales pitch before swapping over. In the second case, the teacher chooses a few groups who come up in turn and perform their speeches, adverts or sales pitches to the rest of the class.

Here is an example to demonstrate the activity:

Example

In the previous lesson students studied the outbreak of the Wars of the Roses.

This event is written on the board alongside such causes as the following:

- The effects of the 100 Years War

- The personality of Henry VI

- The Duke of York's dynastic claims

- The madness of King Henry.

Students would be placed in groups and assigned one of these causes. They would then construct an advert, speech or sales pitch that draws on their previous learning in order to 'sell' the primacy of that particular cause as regards the outbreak of the Wars of the Roses. For example, one group might create a poster advertisement illustrating the various effects of the 100 Years War.

Whichever sales method students choose, they will be synthesising their learning from the lesson in order to create something original and accurate. This process will see them reinforcing their existing knowledge and understanding.

Resources

Here are a set of success criteria for use with this task:

- Ensure that you make it clear to the audience why they should accept your cause as true.

- Look for ways of using persuasive language to draw the audience into accepting your particular cause.

- Use a prop, symbol or dramatic device to make your cause more attractive and believable to the audience.

Teacher's tips

- The activity benefits from being modelled upon its introduction. It is good to give a sales pitch yourself in which you play up the theatricality of the activity and the way in which this dramatic element ought to combine with careful reasoning and persuasive rhetoric.

- If you have a range of causes which differ in complexity, you may wish to decide in advance which groups of students may be best suited to dealing with each cause. This will help ensure all pupils experience success in the starter and can be a way to stretch and challenge students who excel in the subject.

Extensions

- Encourage students to not only sell their own cause but also to critique the other causes. This will strengthen their own case and lead them to consider the relative explanatory power of the other causes.

- If you feel students have sufficient understanding of an event, do not give them the causes. Instead, tell them they must identify what they believe to be the key cause of said event and then sell it accordingly.

- Supplement the activity with peer-assessment. This would entail group's performances being assessed on the grounds of: (i) strength of argument; (ii) accuracy of historical knowledge; and (iii) persuasiveness.

Plenary

Sell your cause

Pupils work in groups to visualise the relationship between an event and its various causes.

Key question: What were the main causes of the Great Depression?

Materials required: Eight pieces of A3 or sugar paper (enough for one per group); a slide containing all the different causes which played a part in the occurrence of the event in question. This is optional – you may want to challenge your students by not providing this.

Activity

This plenary helps students appreciate how a number of different factors can be said to have caused a single event. As such, it is best used when the topic studied during the lesson is an example of this.

Students are put into groups of three or four. Each group is given a large sheet of paper; sugar paper or A3 paper is most suitable. The task is to create a map of the causes which led to the event which has been studied. The map can be designed in a variety of ways:

• The event could be placed in the centre of the paper with the causes coming off this.

• The event could be placed at the far end of the paper with the causes preceding this (like horses racing towards a finish line).

• The event could be placed at the bottom of the paper with the causes falling down towards it.

The advantage of the second two methods is that the relative role the different causes played can be made clear visually. In the second case, the causes which were immediate could be close to the event whilst the long-term causes could be further away. In the third case, the causes which had the biggest impact could be closer to the bottom whilst those that had the lesser impact could be closer to the top.

On the following page is an example to illustrate the activity:

Example

Students have been studying the Great Depression.

The class is split into groups of three or four. Each group has to create a map showing the causes which led to the Depression. They might come up with the following, based on method (ii):

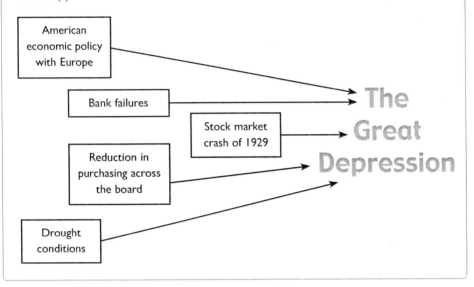

Resources

Indicate to students what you want them to do with each of the causes. For example:

• You must explain each of the causes in detail.

• It should be clear visually which causes you feel were most important.

• You should make connections, where possible, between different causes.

Teacher's tip

The work that students produce in this activity can serve well as either wall displays or revision aids. If you are planning to use it in one of these ways be sure tell students in advance. This will make certain they keep their work to a high standard and take extra care over the creation of their maps.

Extensions

- Create a display area at the front of the room where groups can place their completed maps. Ask students to look at all the maps and to use a Post-It note to leave feedback on a map which they feel is particularly good.

- Collect the completed maps. Redistribute the maps amongst the groups. Ask each group to look at the map they have been given and to identify two good things about it. Go around to each group and ask them to share their positive comments.

- Ask students to include evaluative comments on their maps regarding the relationships between the individual causes and the event.

Starter

What happens next?

Pupils are presented with a little bit of information about the past, and then asked to speculate about what happened next.

Key question: What were the main effects of the 1832 Great Reform Act?

Materials required: A source of narrative description connected to the area of study. This should leave open the question of 'what happened next?'

Activity

This starter centres on speculation. It asks students to apply their existing knowledge so as to make conjectures about the events of the past. These conjectures will precede an exploration of those events, thus forming the basis of the lesson which follows.

Present students with a source or narrative description which leaves open the question of what happened next. Invite them to consider the evidence and to speculate how events unfolded. You should specify that their speculations must be grounded in sound reasoning and connect to the evidence which has been provided, as well as to any prior knowledge which they might possess.

Students should begin by mind-mapping a range of speculations with a partner. They should discuss these before ranking them from most to least likely. The next step is to construct an argument as to why the speculation they deem to be most likely deserves to occupy that position. Finally, pairs are invited to share their results with other pairs, or with the class as a whole (the teacher decides which method to use). In this sharing, it is expected that students advocate on behalf of their speculations and try to convince others as to why they ought to accept them as being highly likely.

On the following page is an example to illustrate the activity:

Example

The lesson is based on the Great Reform Act of 1832.

Students have already studied the period and events leading up to the passing of the act, but have not yet looked at the act itself. A summary of the act is presented, written by someone alive at the time, in which the key points are picked out. Students are invited to speculate as to what happened next, in the period following the passing of the act. They are encouraged to use their knowledge of the period, along with the information about what the act entailed, to inform their speculations.

Resources

To get students thinking about speculation, and to model the type of thought processes which you are looking for, use videos from www.youtube.com featuring animals and sports. Play this up to a certain point and then stop them. Ask students to imagine what might happen next. This will provide them with a simple way in to speculating about the historical events in question.

Teacher's tip

Stress to students the importance of rooting their speculations in reason and evidence. There is the potential for pupils to focus on the creative aspect of the starter and to leave the historical aspect to one side. It would be a shame if such an approach were taken and so you may wish to provide success criteria to help guide students. These could make reference to the both the creative and the historical skills the activity demands.

Extensions

- You may wish to give students a timescale for their speculations. Continuing the example used above, it might be that you ask them to speculate what happened in the immediate aftermath of the act, or events that took place over the following thirty years which could be attributed to the passing of the act.

- Another option is to provide students with categories through which to make their speculations. Continuing from our example above, we might ask students to speculate as to how the act affected Britain's middle classes.

- As students are developing their speculations, walk around the room and question the premises on which propositions are being constructed. This will help students refine their speculations.

Plenary

What happens next?

Pupils use their learning to evaluate the speculations they made at the beginning of the lesson.

Key question: How did the government use propaganda in World War Two?

Materials required: The work produced in the complementary starter; a slide containing step-by-step instructions covering what you want students to do.

Activity

This activity needs to be used in conjunction with its complementary starter. It relies on the work produced in that starter, centring on a comparison between the speculations students have made and what actually turned out to be the case.

Ask students to re-form the pairings that they worked in for the starter and to return to the list of speculations they constructed during that activity. They should go through each speculation in turn and analyse: (a) the reasons why they made that speculation; (b) the validity of that speculation in view of what they have learnt in the lesson; (c) the additional information they think they would have needed in order to make accurate speculations.

Once students have completed their analysis (and it would be best for them to take some notes while they do so) they should form a group of four with another pairing. Each pair should take it in turn to outline the results of their analysis. A discussion should then follow in which students reflect on what they have learnt and how it connects to the original source from which they were expected to speculate. In so doing they will be revisiting the content of the lesson as well as recontextualising the original source.

Here is an example demonstrating the activity:

Example

Students have been studying propaganda in World War Two.

At the beginning of the lesson they were presented with a British Government poster from the time and invited to speculate about its purpose, reception, production and intended audience. In pairs, students would work through these speculations, analysing them in light of what they have learnt during the lesson. It is likely that they will identify a lack of depth and nuance in their speculations and will be able to rectify this through the application of their new knowledge. Subsequent discussion could touch on this as well as on other findings.

Resources

Use the following evaluation tips to help students assess their speculations:

• Look for the strengths and weaknesses in your work.

• Think about how your work compares to what you now know.

• Consider how likely and reasonable the ideas you put forward were.

Teacher's tip

This activity is heavily dependent on students having produced a reasonably long list of speculations in the starter (a minimum of five items). When students are first coming up with their speculations, walk around the room and ensure that the lists they are producing are of sufficient length. If they are not, make it clear to students that they need to think of more things to add. This will help make certain that each pair has enough material to analyse in the plenary, making the activity worthwhile for all involved.

Extensions

• Students swap their list of speculations with another pair. They then complete the activity as outlined above, except that they will be using the different set of speculations. On completion they report their findings to the pair whose speculations they have been analysing.

• Challenge students to produce some guidelines which they could use in the future in order to make more accurate speculations.

• Ask students to identify the key pieces of information from the lesson which they feel a person would need in order to be able to speculate accurately about what it was that took place.

Starter

What is the connection?

Challenge pupils to use their reasoning skills to connect different items from the past.

Key question: How significant was Robert Owen's contribution to the Industrial Revolution?

Materials required: A hand-out containing two things related to the period of study. These should be connected in some way, but you should withhold the nature of this connection.

Activity

In this activity students are presented with two things from the past which possess some kind of connection. The connection, however, is withheld from the students and they must speculate as to what it might be. They are expected to use their knowledge of the topic being studied, as well as sound reasoning, to advance connections which they believe likely to be proved true.

You may choose to present students with two events separated by time and space. It is explained that there is a connection between the first event and the second event. Students have to speculate what the connection might be.

Another option is to introduce students to an event, time period or theme and then to show them an object or item which is somehow connected to this. It is up to the students to speculate what the connection is.

Finally, you may choose to present a written source of some sort and ask students to speculate how it connects to the period or theme which you and they are currently studying. In each of the approaches outlined it is up to you to judge how much help students may require. This might come in the form of contextualising information or general hints about the paths pupils might want to explore in order to make their speculations.

On the following page is an example of the activity in action:

Example

Students have been studying the Industrial Revolution.

As they enter the room, there is a picture of Robert Owen's model factory set-up at New Lanark on the board. This is accompanied by a hand-out carrying further images showing different aspects of the site. Students are asked to speculate what the connection might be between the pictures and the Industrial Revolution. Alternatively, students are given information about Robert Owen's beliefs, alongside the pictures, and then asked to use these to make their speculations.

In both cases, pupils are immediately engaged with the lesson and with the topic of study. In addition, they are given every chance to succeed; the aim is to make reasonable arguments based on the information to hand, rather than to necessarily fall on the correct answer. This way, every pupil can experience success and feel motivated at the start of the lesson.

Resources

Here are some really useful websites for getting source information to use in this activity:

- www.british-history.ac.uk

- www.hartford-hwp.com

- www.eyewitnesstohistory.com

- www.historicaltextarchive.com

- tps.stanford.edu

Teacher's tip

It is important to get the balance right between revealing too little and revealing too much. In the case of the former, students are likely to disengage because the difficulty level is too high. In the case of the latter, students will not have to engage in a great deal of reasoning or analysis because the connection(s) will be obvious. You may need to experiment with the amount of information you reveal before you get the balance right.

Extensions

- Drip-feed information to students. Each time you reveal a little more, ask students to reconsider their speculations and decide whether they wish to alter them or not.

- Provide all students with the same main information (like the picture on the board in the example above) but then give different students different ancillary information. Ask them to speculate based on the information they have. Students could then share speculations and look at how the ancillary information has influenced people's thinking.

- Ask students to come up with a procedure to test the validity of their speculations. This could be followed through in the remainder of the lesson.

Plenary

What is the connection?

Pupils use their learning to connect together the different causes and consequences linked to the topic.

Key question: Why did the Normans win the Battle of Hastings?

Materials required: A slideshow containing a range of causes and consequences which connect to the lesson; these could all be on the same slide, or you could divide them up and show them on consecutive slides.

Activity

Present students with a range of causes and consequences connected to what has been studied during the lesson. These could be presented all at once, in groups, or sequentially. Ask students to make the connection between each cause or consequence and the area of study.

The plenary can be conducted in a quick-fire manner, with the teacher revealing the causes and consequences on the board before asking students to make their connections as swiftly as they can. Alternatively, students could work in pairs or groups to make a series of connections. In this latter case, the teacher would draw the activity to a close by asking a number of pairs or groups to share their connections with the rest of the class.

The activity will result in students reviewing and revisiting what they have learnt, as well as using it actively in order to make connections. These ought to be explanatory in nature, demonstrating how and why the cause or consequence connects to the area of study. It will not be enough to give a simple connection (A was caused by B). The point is to explain the connections, making use of sound reasoning in order to do so.

Here is an example to illustrate the activity:

Example

The area of study is the Battle of Hastings.

To introduce the main enquiry exploring why the Normans won the battle, students are presented with a collection of causes which purport to explain why the battle took place (including why it took place when and where it did). Working in groups, they have a few minutes to connect each cause to their knowledge and to create an explanation as to why that connection ought to be considered to be the case. The teacher then chooses a couple of groups to provide feedback for each cause. If there is enough time, a collection of consequences can then be examined, following the same approach.

Resources

You can provide pupils with a pro-forma such as the following which they use to make their connections:

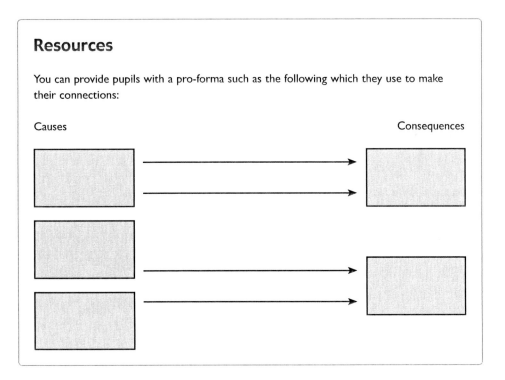

Teacher's tips

- The scope of the activity is limited if students do not support their connections with analysis and explanation. It is important to model the type of responses you expect from students and to highlight why this is necessary and why giving a simple connection is not sufficient.

- If students struggle to make connections, encourage them to discuss their ideas with other members of the class. Encourage students to speak to peers sat away from them, or to those who are working in different groups. Another perspective is likely to stimulate new thinking on the matter in hand.

Extensions

- Challenge students to make connections between causes and consequences. This will require a chain of reasoning. Students will have to explain why the cause connects to the event, why the event connects to the consequence, and why the cause and consequence connect to each other via the event.

- Provide students with a variety of short-term and long-term causes or consequences. This will help broaden their thinking on the subject as well as challenge them to use different styles of reasoning.

- Ask students to make horizontal connections. These will either be between causes or between consequences. Such a task will help students to identify themes and motifs which may underpin the various factors and results.

Section 7
Enquiry

Starter

Mystery

Invoke the power of mystery to engage and inspire your students.

Key question: Why did people believe in Witchcraft?

Materials required: A mystery of some sort. This could be an unusual object, a document or picture without any contextualising information or something else entirely; ideally, you should have a mystery of which you can bring in many copies (one for each group).

Activity

Encourage students to start enquiring by presenting them with some kind of mystery. This ought to be designed such that it will draw their attention and be amenable to further investigation. It should not be something that students can unravel quickly. It may be that you give students a mystery to which it would be very difficult to find the correct answer. That is fine. The answers students do come up with can be shared, discussed and tested for potential validity. The enquiry can then continue through the lesson, with additional resources brought in as you go along.

There are a number of different ways in which you can present a mystery. It could be in the form of an object (or a series of objects, different groups receiving different ones) which students will not have encountered before. This could be presented inside a box or a bag to further heighten the sense of mystery. It could also be in the form of a source, such as a document or a picture, which is presented without any contextualising information. Finally, it could be in the form of an event, a happening or a person's action. The mystery in this case is why the said thing came to pass in the first place.

Here is an example of the activity in action:

Example

Let us imagine pupils are studying the history of witchcraft and this is the first lesson.

Sit students in groups of three or four when they enter the classroom. Give each group a worksheet, on which is printed a set of prosecutor's charges against an alleged witch. The groups read through the worksheet and discuss what they think it is about and what has led to its creation. The class comes back together and discusses their ideas. The lesson progresses along the line of enquiry: 'What is this document and why is it important?' or something similar (students could decide for themselves what will be the specific enquiry).

Resources

It is well worth your while collecting a variety of mysterious objects over the course of a few years. Aim to get a third of your objects in the first year – each one being relevant for a specific topic which you teach. Get another third in the second year and the final third the year after that. This way, you will gradually build up a collection of mysterious objects you can use to inspire and engage your pupils.

Teacher's tip

Choose your mysteries carefully. Consider the prior learning of your students and their current ability levels. Do not be afraid to include contextual information if you think a mystery on its own will prove too difficult. It is better to ensure all students find success in the activity than to risk some becoming disengaged for whatever reason.

Extensions

- Once students have come up with some tentative ideas to explain their mystery, they choose which they feel is the most likely and write a defence of this, using reasoning and examples to make their case

- Bring in a variety of different mysteries. These could be set up at different stations around the room or passed from group to group. Students look at each mystery in turn, making notes as they go.

- Bring in a variety of different mysteries but allow each group to see only one. They must analyse their mystery and then conduct an enquiry through the lesson with the explanation of that mystery as their focus. Findings are shared by everybody in the plenary.

Plenary

Mystery

Challenge students to develop a mystery-based starter which calls on the learning they have done in the lesson.

Key question: Has Henry VI been harshly judged by historians?

Materials required: A slide containing a set of criteria structuring what you are asking students to do.

Activity

Ask students to plan a mystery starter that could be used to introduce the topic which has been covered during the lesson. Give a set of criteria which must be met in order for the starter to be both appropriate and sufficiently mysterious. Such criteria might include:

- The starter should include something to do with the topic we have studied.

- Something should be chosen which, without further information, appears to be something of a mystery.

- It should be clear how you want future students to engage with that mystery.

Once students have planned their mystery starter, they should provide a rationale as to why they have planned it as they have. In addition, they should indicate how they would teach the rest of the lesson, demonstrating how this would connect to the starter (including how it would lead to the mystery being unravelled).

The beauty of this plenary is that it causes students to think about that which they have studied in a number of different ways. First, they must revisit what they have learnt. Second, they must look at what they have learnt in the context of whether it could be used for a mystery or not. Third, they must synthesise some of the material so as to create the starter. Fourth, they must consider that synthesis analytically so as to produce a defence of it. Fifth, they must plan how their starter will connect to everything else which has been studied.

Here is an example demonstrating how the activity works:

Example

Students have been studying the reign of Henry VI.

In constructing a mystery starter they might provide a layout of King's College Chapel in Cambridge without any annotations. They would then invite future students to suggest what the image represented and how it might connect to Henry VI. The rationale could be that the Chapel signifies many of the influences on and interests of Henry VI and so acts as a good starting point. The rest of the lesson could connect with different elements of Henry's reign through different aspects of the Chapel and the intentions which led to its being founded.

Resources

Provide pupils with the following success criteria to help them construct their starter:

• Think about your audience.

• Ensure you make the starter mysterious, but also accessible.

• Work out how your starter will lead into the rest of the lesson.

Teacher's tip

If you have begun the lesson using a mystery starter of your own, then students will be able to use that as a model for their own work. If, however, you have not done this, then you will need to explain what is required in detail, or model an example at the beginning of the plenary. Upon repeating the activity, such modelling is likely to become unnecessary as a growing sense of familiarity develops and students understand in advance what is expected of them.

Extensions

- Put students in groups and give each group something from the lesson which they must use to construct a mystery starter. The challenge here is that students cannot choose that which they might view as being easiest.

- When students have finished constructing their mystery starters (and you will have to decide if these are to be done individually, in pairs or in groups) ask them to swap with someone else and to have a go at completing the starter they have created.

- Challenge students to anticipate the different responses their mystery starter may elicit.

Starter

You decide

Give students the chance to decide how they will go about investigating a particular topic.

Key question: Were working conditions in nineteenth-century Lancashire poor for everyone?

Materials required: A collection of resources connected to the topic. These should be photocopied and stapled together into small resource packs. You can either create one per student, or one per pair of students.

Activity

This starter asks students to decide for themselves the line of enquiry they will pursue through the lesson. It gets them thinking like historians: they must look at the information which is to hand and make a decision as to what question(s) it is worth trying to answer.

Present students with a collection of material. It would be good to make sure this includes a range of different source types and a selection of viewpoints concerning whatever topic you are studying. Students look through the material, either individually or in pairs, and decide what they think is most interesting. Once they have settled on something, they come up with a question of enquiry which is linked to it and which they would like to answer. This question forms the basis of their learning in the rest of the lesson. They either work independently on the question, or complete the activities you have planned with their question in mind. At the end of the lesson, students can reflect on whether their enquiry has been successful or not and the reasons behind this.

Here is an example to illustrate how the activity works:

Example

The topic is working conditions in nineteenth-century Lancashire.

Students are given a collection of materials which includes: a picture of a cotton mill; an account of life at work from the perspective of a child; an account of life at work from the perspective of a foreman; some figures regarding cotton production during the period; an extract from a speech made by someone calling for factory reform. Such materials could be kept short so that students can get through them quickly.

Pupils go through all the sources, analysing and investigating each one in turn. When they have been through them all, they decide which source they think is the most interesting. Returning to this one, they begin to think of some possible questions they could ask of it. Finally, they settle on a single enquiry-question they would like to pursue.

Resources

Here are some example enquiry questions, based on the working conditions in nineteenth-century Lancashire:

- What was life like for children in mills?

- Why was cotton so important?

- Who made money from selling all this cotton?

You might want to provide pupils with some sample enquiry questions as a way to help them access the task.

Teacher's tip

This starter will work well with topics which have scope for exploration in various directions. A straightforward cause-and-effect issue might not have enough in it to merit the kind of approach outlined. More discursive subjects, such as the *nature* of something (like working conditions in a period), will give students a greater range of options from which to choose. Such topics are more likely to lead to a range of different enquiry questions being developed. This will help create more of a sense of independence for your learners.

Extensions

- When students have settled on their enquiry question, ask them to share their decision with five of their peers. Explain they can modify their question as a result of doing this, if they so wish.

- Ask students to come up with a list of sub-questions they believe they will need to answer in order to discover the answer to their enquiry question.

- When students have settled on their enquiry question, ask them to team up with peers who have a similar or related question. The groups which form work together during the lesson to try and answer their questions.

Plenary

You decide

Students evaluate their own enquiries and then share their findings with their peers; just like real-life academics.

Key question: How did Peter the Great rule Russia?

Materials required: Work produced during the lesson; a slide containing step-by-step instructions explaining what students are to do.

Activity

This activity needs to be used in conjunction with its complementary starter. It has two parts which, whilst standing separate, do have a clear connection.

- Part 1: Students review what they have done during the lesson based on the question of enquiry they came up with in the starter. This review can take whatever form you wish, although it should culminate in students assessing whether or not they are in a position to answer their question. If they are, they should produce a written answer which makes use of what they have learnt in the lesson. If they are not, they should analyse what they *have* learnt and identify what gaps exist in their knowledge and why this has led them to not be able to answer their question. Finally, they should suggest what further study they need to do in order to produce an answer.

- Part 2: Students present their findings to other individuals, pairs or groups. They explain what their line of enquiry was and whether or not they have an answer to their question. They should then explain their answer, using information from the lesson in so doing, or outline why they do not have an answer and how they would go about reaching one if they were given more time and resources.

The two parts together echo the research process which forms the basis of academic study in the West.

Here is an example of how the activity works:

Example

The topic of study is the reign of Peter the Great of Russia.

Let us imagine that from the material presented to the class during the starter, one group of students has come up with the question: 'How did Peter the Great affect the cultural life of Russia during his reign?' The plenary would see this group reviewing what they did in the lesson in order to assess whether they were in a position to answer the question or not. They would then follow one of the two paths outlined above, before sharing their findings with another group (who would in turn share their findings with them).

The whole process sees pupils revisiting and reinforcing their learning. As a result, they will secure the knowledge and understanding which they have developed during the course of the lesson.

Resources

Here are some questions which pupils can use during their discussion with other groups:

- What was your question?

- How did you go about researching the question?

- What would you say are your key findings?

- What are the causes and consequences of your key findings?

- Where would you take your research next if you had the opportunity?

Teacher's tip

When first using this starter-plenary combination with your classes, you may want to help students to form their questions and line of enquiry. This will allow you to direct them toward areas and approaches which you know will be fruitful and which you anticipate it will be easier for them to answer. When students are familiar with how the activities work, you can step back and give them a freer reign.

Extensions

- Challenge students to include a self-assessment in their review. This should focus on what they themselves have done in the lesson and the extent to which that has contributed (or not) to their ability to answer the question they posed.

- Once students have dealt with their own question, ask them to take on the question of another individual, pair or group and to see if they can answer that (and if not, to identify what they would need to study in order to be able to do so).

- Ask students to assess the strengths and weaknesses of the question or line of enquiry they came up with in the starter.

Starter

Different paths

Students work in groups, with each group following a different line of enquiry into the topic.

Key question: What were the main effects of The Great Depression?

Materials required: A set of number cards for creating groups. For example, the numbers 1-7 printed out and cut up four times; a slide containing the same number of paths of enquiries as there are numbers (for example, seven paths).

Activity

Before your class arrives, work out how many groups you want to divide them into. I would always suggest groups of three or four students. Once you have done this, print off and cut out some numbers so that each group is represented by the equivalent number of numbers. For example, if you have decided on seven groups of four then print off and cut out four number ones, four number twos, four number threes and so on. As students enter the room, hand these out at random.

Place on the board seven paths of enquiry (or enough for one per group) which are numbered one to seven. When your class have sat down, explain that they need to find out who is in their group (the students who have the same numbers), team up with them, write down what enquiry they have been given and come up with a short plan of action for pursuing that enquiry. This plan of action will then form the basis of what students do in the main part of the lesson, where they will be researching and investigating the line of enquiry they have been given.

Here is an example illustrating how the activity works:

> ## Example
>
> The topic of study is the Great Depression.
>
> The class contains twenty students. Divide the students into five groups of four. The following paths of enquiry are displayed on the board:

1 How influential was the Great Crash?

2 Did the large number of bank closures in the 1930s cause the depression?

3 What role did consumers play in the depression?

4 Were the Government to blame?

5 How important were environmental and population factors?

Each group pursues one of these. The starter is vital in setting them up us a group and ensuring they plan how they will approach their particular enquiry. As in this example here, different paths will require different approaches.

The teacher should give groups guidance and support in fleshing out their method of enquiry. This will ensure they are able to succeed in what they doing, and that they do not encounter obstacles which are insurmountable.

Resources

Here are some success criteria which pupils can use to help them come up with an appropriate plan of enquiry:

- Work out what you think are the most important things you need to investigate.

- Come up with a set of sub-questions you can use to structure your research.

- Put the sub-questions into the order you think is most appropriate.

Extensions

- If students are not happy with the path of enquiry they have been given, encourage them to come up with their own. Check this and, if you are in agreement, let them investigate it instead of the one you suggested.

- When students have come up with their plans, ask one member of each group to act as an envoy. They go to other groups and explain their group's plan, receiving feedback on its strengths and weaknesses. The envoy then returns to their original group and recounts what they have heard.

- Groups are asked to analyse how they think their path of enquiry might connect to the other paths. This could lead to some groups working together on certain parts of their investigations.

Plenary

Different paths

Groups share the results of their investigations, helping everyone in the class to develop a broad understanding of the topic.

Key question: What were the main effects of the Great Depression?

Materials required: Work done during the lesson, based on the starting point provided by the complementary starter; sheets of A3 or sugar paper, enough for one per group.

Activity

This plenary should be used in conjunction with the starter of the same name. In that starter, students are randomly allocated a line of enquiry. They work in groups, pursuing this through the course of the lesson.

Ask students to prepare a short presentation outlining the line of enquiry on which they have been working and the results of their investigations. This presentation should be constructed in line with pre-defined success criteria. I would suggest the following:

• Summarise your findings and present them clearly and concisely.

• Explain how they connect to your line of enquiry.

• Indicate whether your findings are conclusive or if further study is required. If the latter is the case, suggest what further study should be undertaken.

These criteria could be expanded to cover form (use drama as part of your presentation), involvement (every member of the group must add something to the presentation) and wider thinking (demonstrate how your findings connect to what you have been studying this term).

When students are ready, ask each group to come to the front and present their findings in turn. If there is not sufficient time to do this, ask groups to pair up and to present to each other instead. A brief selection of key points could then be shared with the class as a whole.

Here is an example illustrating how the activity works:

Example

The topic of study is the Great Depression.

The class contains twenty students. We divide them into five groups of four. The following paths of enquiry are displayed on the board:

1   How influential was the Great Crash?

2   Did the large number of bank closures in the 1930s cause the depression?

3   What role did consumers play in the depression?

4   Were the Government to blame?

5   How important were environmental and population factors?

This is the same as is noted above for the complementary starter. By asking groups to present their findings in turn, every student in the class will gain some insight into each of the lines of enquiry. Further, they will be able to make connections which would be difficult to observe through studying the areas sequentially.

In addition, every student will have the opportunity to reinforce their own learning during the course of their presentation. This will help them to secure the knowledge and understanding they have developed during the course of the lesson.

Resources

Here are some success criteria for pupils to use when presenting their findings:

*   Pick out your key findings and begin by explaining these.

*   Provide some background to your key findings, indicating why they are the case.

*   Try to connect your key findings together; show any patterns or themes which emerge.

Teacher's tip

Keep the criteria for the presentations highly specific. This will ensure that students do not present their findings in an amorphous way that lacks clarity. Identify groups who are meeting the criteria (during the preparation process) and highlight what they are doing (and why it is good) to the rest of the class.

Extensions

• Ask students to peer-assess the presentations. This could be in the form of three things which were good (including explanations of why they were good) and one thing which could be improved (including an explanation of how that improvement ought to be made and why it would constitute an improvement).

• Challenge students to include comparisons across time or thematic comparisons in their presentations. This will involve them looking at their line of enquiry in wider historical context.

• Give students an unusual medium through which they must convey their findings. For example: poetry, musical theatre or mime.